EDUCATION MATTERS

General Editor: Ted Wragg

DRAMA IN THE CURRIC

BOOKS IN THIS SERIES

DRAMA IN THE CURRICULUM

John Somers

CASSELL

Cassell Educational Limited

Villiers House	387 Park Avenue South
41/47 Strand	New York
London	NY 10016–8810
WC2N 5JE	

British Library Cataloguing-in-Publication Data
A catalogue record for this book is available from the British Library.

ISBN: 0–304–32594–5 (hardback)
0–304–32589–9 (paperback)

Typeset by Litho Link Ltd, Welshpool, Powys

Printed and bound in Great Britain by
Redwood Books, Trowbridge, Wilts.

CONTENTS

This book is dedicated to Ken Scott, teacher, mentor, philosopher and humanitarian.

FOREWORD

Professor E.C. Wragg, Exeter University

During the 1980s a succession of Education Acts changed considerably the nature of schools and their relationships with the outside world. Parents were given more rights and responsibilities, including the opportunity to serve on the governing body of their child's school. The 1988 Education Reform Act in particular, by introducing for the first time a National Curriculum, the testing of children at the ages of 7, 11, 14 and 16, local management, including financial responsibility and the creation of new types of school, was a radical break with the past. Furthermore the disappearance of millions of jobs, along with other changes in our society, led to reforms not only of schools, but also of further and higher education.

In the wake of such rapid and substantial changes it was not just parents and lay people, but also teachers and other professionals working in education, who found themselves struggling to keep up with what these many changes meant and how to get the best out of them. The *Education Matters* series addresses directly the major topics of reform, such as the new curriculum, testing and assessment, the role of parents and the handling of school finances, considering their effects on primary, secondary, further and higher education, and also the continuing education of adults.

The aim of the series is to present information about the challenges facing education in the remainder of the twentieth century in an authoritative but readable form. The books in the series, therefore, are of particular interest to parents, governors and all those concerned with education, but are written in such a way as to give an overview to students, experienced teachers and other professionals who work in the field.

Each book gives an account of the relevant legislation and background, but, more importantly, stresses practical implications of change with specific examples of what is being or can be done to make reforms work effectively. The authors are not only authorities in their field, but also have direct experience of the matters they write about. That is why the *Education Matters* series makes an important contribution to both debate and practice.

ACKNOWLEDGEMENTS

Students of Exeter University: 'When I Was a Boy' on pp.163–174 (Katie Aldwinkle, Rachel Webster, Tina Davies, Gail Dick, Emma Saunders, Jane Guswell and Julia Pearn); 'I Wish We Were There' on pp.174–184 (Lorraine Moore, Alison Moore, Lorraine Bushen, Lisa Pearson, Karen Stephens, Lindsay Ryan and Sarah Were).

Teachers at Exwick Middle School; especially Carolyn Ballard, Elaine Hennessy, Gary Read, Gill Palmer, Ken Turner and Nicky Hobbs.

Freelance radio producer, Andy Hitchcock, Devon County Council Media Studies Adviser, Tim Arnold, and University of Exeter Technician, John Staplehurst.

Photography by Brian Merrick, Lecturer at Exeter University, and Tony Fisher; photographs processed at Exeter University Photographic Unit. Graphics by Kirsty Sumner, Neil Bollen and Maddy Lavender.

For their support and help: Bill Stanton, Paddy Creber, Geoff Fox and Cherry Dodwell and the many subject colleagues who read and checked the National Curriculum sections of the book.

PREFACE

In watching the performance of the play in the local community centre, amidst proud parents and interested local people, in the very school-room where some of the original incidents had occurred, what came across very strongly was the children's sense of ownership of what they were doing. The odd word forgotten, or scene changes muddled, made little difference because from first to last the child actors showed in their movements and language that they knew what this play was about. Because they had this confidence in the meaning of what they were doing, they were very success- ful in moving their audience to laughter and tears. An added layer of significance for the adult audience came from the realisation that, in acting out scenes from the history of their forebears, these children were themselves becoming the possessors of their own cultural heritage and making another piece of local history to be remembered. (Fox, 1990)

A performance which communicates, through the art form, the insights and understandings which have accrued to young people through researching, sifting, shaping and presenting exciting material, can be one of the most thrilling events in the life of a school. In the case of the Exwick project, described in Chapter 10 of this book, the performances were significant because they came through a process in which teachers operated at the highest professional level, radiating that professionalism through material and learning structures which caught the imagination and interest of the young people in their charge. The work was a celebration of what teachers can achieve when they co-operate in the company of well-motivated students.

Whatever curriculum is in place, there must be room for projects of this nature. They represent education at its best and, although their components can be described in National Curriculum terms, they transcend the coolness of ring-binder description to live as resounding testimonies to the best that confidently applied teacher skill and ingenuity can achieve. They are built on the foundation of good curriculum practice, including the generality of drama teaching where the aim is not to produce material for performance.

Not all of this book explicitly addresses 'National Curriculum matters'. It looks at most facets of drama teaching and, through the material of three of its chapters, shows how drama can be a vibrant part of the new curriculum. Experienced drama teachers may find it a useful reference work, checking out their current practice against the 'skills', 'techniques' and 'role of the teacher' sections. Guidance given on drama and other subjects, and drama as the focus for cross-curricular projects, may help them in furthering links between the subject and the rest of the curriculum. The book may also be of use to less experienced teachers of drama, or those who wish to use drama approaches, but are not sure where to start or how to progress. Finally it may form a basic reader for student teachers who want to know how drama can be taught within the National Curriculum. I hope it will inspire teachers in all phases of education to consider how drama, in its many guises, might enhance the learning experiences of their students.

I have written in simple terms in an attempt to demystify the components of drama learning and teaching. I have not used illustrative examples from all phases as I feel many of the models given may be adapted upwards or downwards to suit a particular age. I use the term 'educational drama' to mark out from other forms the drama which takes place in schools. Throughout I refer to all learners as 'students' whether they be infants or university students. To avoid the clumsy use of she/he, her/his, I have tried to use gender-specific terms in equal measure.

References to the National Curriculum will become dated as yet more changes are made to its format and content. My hope is that the examples culled from the version in place at the time of writing will continue to serve as useful models of drama's place in our schools.

Chapter 1

INTRODUCTION

Drama and its place in the National Curriculum

The Second World War acted as a watershed for change which affected many areas of British life. Britain had secured victory at great cost, and as they coped with post-war austerity the British people made clear they wanted change. New house-building programmes, a proper social security system, a National Health Service and the nationalization of important utilities were designed to bring about conditions which would improve the lot of all families. A new social-democratic consensus emerged which was to survive until the rise of Thatcherism in the 1980s.

The 1944 Education Act had laid the foundations for a system that would remedy the waste of talent and rigidity which characterized most pre-war schools. The new Labour 'landslide' Government and its advisers were intent on providing a healthier, more rounded and better-quality experience for the country's children. The 1933 Hadow Report on the primary school had already provided a framework within which this iconoclastic development could take place. The introduction to the report clearly signalled the Committee's view of much current primary practice and the kind of change it would like to see:

> A school is at once a physical environment, a training ground of the mind, and a spiritual society. Are we satisfied that in each of these respects the primary schools of today are all that, with the knowledge and resources at our command, we have the power to make them? . . . Is their curriculum humane and realistic, unencumbered by the dead wood of formal tradition, quickened by enquiry and experiment, and inspired not by an attachment to conventional orthodoxies, but by a vivid appreciation of the needs and possibilities of the children themselves? Are the methods of organisation and the character of their equipment, the scale on which they are staffed, and the lines on which their education is planned, of a kind best calculated to encourage individual work and persistent practical activity among pupils, initiative and originality among teachers, and to foster in both the spirit which leaves the beaten path and strikes fearlessly into new fields, which is the soul of education? (Board of Education, 1931, p.xiv)

Figure 1.1 Boys dancing, Steward Street School, Birmingham, 1948

The arts found a ready place in this new climate and experiment abounded. HMI scoured the country looking for models of good practice, broadcasting them widely through courses, demonstration and pamphlets. A particularly significant pamphlet was *Story of a School* (Ministry of Education, 1949), from which the photograph in Figure 1.1 is taken. The arts were embraced as ideal media for pupil-centred learning and freedom of expression. The most rapid development took place in our primary schools, but the right of all secondary students to experience the arts was enhanced with the widespread introduction of comprehensive education. During the 1960s and 1970s, schools nurtured a wide range of artistic activity and innovation.

By the early 1980s drama was commonly used in both secondary and primary phases. At this time, however, the government signalled its ambivalence by virtually stopping the training of secondary drama teachers within the undergraduate programme. In 1989 the consultation documents on the National Curriculum indicated that drama was not to be recognized as a separate subject, but was to be subsumed within English. There seemed something arbitrary about this – music and art were included as discrete subjects, while drama and dance were subsumed in English and PE respectively. Those who had read the political runes were not surprised. Drama was characterized by the Right as a creature of the 'progressive sixties', child-centred and without a recognized body of knowledge to be transmitted. A subject which was responsive to students' concerns, which aimed to provide a forum for speculative consideration of some of the most important issues of our time, but which had no obvious connection with the world of work, was viewed with suspicion: 'The Right is concerned with facts and the status quo and wish to emphasise "what is" rather than "what might be" which is potentially subversive' (Lawton, 1992, p.17).

The National Curriculum was introduced in haste with an insulting absence of proper consultation with teachers and HMI. Denis Lawton comments:

> when the curriculum sections of the Education Reform Bill were written, HMI expertise and experience were ignored, and a National Curriculum was produced which was based simply on the list of subjects which education ministers and their civil servants had presumably studied at school. . . .There was little difference between the National Curriculum 1988 and the curriculum stipulated in the 1904 Secondary Regulations. (Lawton, 1992, p.49)

Little or no research had been carried out into possible structures and content, with the result that state schools took part in a gigantic, national pilot study. Problems soon emerged – science attainment targets were reduced from seventeen to four and testing restricted to the core subjects, for example, and curriculum overload led the government to declare music and art non-statutory at Key Stage 4. Primary teachers have found it impossible to implement the curriculum as currently envisaged, so just three years after its introduction, a major review of its application in that age range was undertaken. Some educationalists fear that admired British primary practice, developed through an exciting and sustained period of educational change, will be adversely affected by the National Curriculum's prescriptiveness, and the uncertainty and upheaval that surround its implementation: 'the greatest danger we face is that our primary schools will lose confidence in the very reforms which have brought visitors from all over the world to see them, and will be afraid to stray from the paths that lead to the tests' (Joan Sallis, in Black, 1992, p.66).

The teaching of English is to receive fresh examination and the testing systems at 7, 11, and 14 are set to move closer to the 'paper and pencil' tests which right-wing educationalists wanted at the outset.

Successive ministers of education have sought to undermine the role of the teacher as professional. Teachers find that their prime responsibility – planning their students' curriculum – has been considerably reduced. National Curriculum documents speak of teachers 'delivering the curriculum', terminology which suggests it has originated and been packaged elsewhere. Brian Cox, chair of the original working party on English, co-author of the Black Papers which questioned 'progressive' education and no friend of the supposed 'trendy lefties' who, the Conservative Right is convinced, pervade our schools, states:

> particularly after Kenneth Clarke's period of office as education secretary, Conservatives have been making wild, vituperative attacks on the teaching profession which have seriously undermined morale. Teachers in state education are underpaid, overworked and often exhausted. (Cox, 1992)

Government has acquired wide-ranging new powers through successive acts of Parliament. The Education Bill published in October 1992, the seventeenth piece of educational legislation since 1979, encouraged more schools to seek grant-maintained status, limited the power of local authorities and introduced the concept of 'sponsors' who, through a contribution of at least 10 per cent of the cost of setting up a new school, will be able to claim four governor appointments. The Secretary of State acquired 44 new powers when the Act passed through Parliament (DES, 1992a).

Teachers will not be encouraged by the assertion, contained in the White Paper which preceded the Bill, that 'parents know better than educational theorists and administrators' (DES, 1992b), a statement without proper foundation, as teachers have constant recourse to theory. In this respect, the White Paper's view is in stark contrast to the sentiments of the Hadow Report quoted above, and those of Dominic Milroy, headteacher of Ampleforth College and chairman of the Headmasters' Conference:

> The fact remains, however, that the professional achievement of teachers continues to be huge, and that there is no professional body which knows, collectively, more about teaching than teachers do. This should not be surprising. What is surprising is that teachers have been asked to play so small a role in current educational reforms. (Black, 1992, p.60)

Local authorities are being weakened and their responsibility for the education service eroded. Government tells us this will free schools from the yoke of local government, but sceptics point out that with the local education authorities out of the way, dictates from the centre can proceed unimpeded. Even senior Conservative politicians have voiced their disquiet on this front. In *The Times Educational Supplement* (4 December 1992) Sir Malcolm Thornton, Conservative chairman of the Commons Select Committee on Education, feels that the idea of grant-maintained schools 'owes more to the antipathy of national government to local authorities than to finding the best way to improve education.'

Many have some sympathy for the teacher who said on 6 September of the same year: 'I have been in the job for so long now that I know that if you just sit tight and carry on doing the things you ought to be doing, all these stupid people with hare-brained ideas will go away in the end' (*Observer Schools Report*).

Throughout 1992, the government was faced with implacable resistance from most teachers and many parents to key aspects of the National Curriculum. In April 1993 John Patten, the Education Secretary, asked Sir Ron Dearing to conduct a review which would focus on four key questions:

• What is the scope for slimming down the curriculum itself?
• How can the testing arrangements themselves be simplified?
• What is the future of the 10-level scale for graduating pupils' progress?
• How can the central administration of the National Curriculum and testing arrangements be improved?

If implemented, many of the recommendations in Sir Ron's interim report will go a long way to placating professional opposition (NCC, 1993). Among other things, it recommends a slimmer, less tightly prescribed curriculum with some of the current content becoming optional, with time freed for work of teachers' own choice, ranging from 10–15 per cent in infant classes to 20–25 per cent at Key Stage 3. This flexibility of time usage could create opportunities for drama activity to be properly covered and space for the kind of cross-curricular project described in Chapter 10 to flourish. The recommendations will, after proper consultation, be implemented in September 1995 or September 1996. In the interim period, the curriculum, as presently constituted, will apply.

And what of drama's place in all this? It remains a vibrant force within many schools. In 1992 approximately 70 per cent of secondary schools in England and Wales had a drama teacher and in 1990, 46,000 students entered the GCSE drama examination (ACGB, 1992). Through its inclusion in English, drama must be taught by law. In addition, the 1988 Education Reform Act requires school curricula to be 'balanced and broadly based' (DES, 1988). The government has expressly stated that the foundation subjects are not a complete curriculum, and this gives schools the flexibility to include drama in addition to the legal requirement.

Although drama has a statutory place in the National Curriculum, many feel it is not described in ways which allow it to thrive. An experienced headteacher of a middle school believes it is ascribed little more than a service role:

> I would . . . argue that primary school children may well not progress in drama at all if it is understood in terms implied by the National Curriculum; that is to say, as a subject which exists to serve other subjects which, by implication, are more important. (Winston, 1991, pp.7–9)

I am a little more optimistic. Drama has the ability to place material in a detailed human context and it has much to offer in this regard across the curriculum. Numerous references in the subject documents to the use of drama suggest there are opportunities for it to flourish and be taught with integrity. It can also play a central role in bringing teachers and students together to carry through work which transcends the isolation of compartmentalized subject teaching, celebrating the best of creative practice. It is the purpose of this book to show how this may be achieved. Its content is based on the premise that drama and the arts in general have an indispensable role within our culture and that this must be reflected within the curricula of our educational establishments. It is the right of individuals to learn about the arts and to have the opportunity to become skilled practitioners of their languages. Whilst I can be positive about drama's place in the National Curriculum, it is my hope that we are conducting something of an interim holding operation during which we need to ensure that drama does not wither on the educational vine before a more enlightened government recognizes the worst aspects of the current National Curriculum model and returns the arts to their proper place in our schools.

We shall look first at the nature and uniqueness of the dramatic experience and at the skills that students must acquire if they are to develop and control their use of the medium. An examination of the role of teachers of drama and the approaches they may employ is followed by an appraisal of the place of text in drama, leading naturally to consideration of communication through the medium and the function of performance. A systematic assessment of drama's ability to play a significant part in the teaching of all National Curriculum subjects precedes an examination of how it can act as a catalyst for cross-curricular projects. The final chapter describes such a project carried out in a middle school.

Chapter 2

THE NATURE OF DRAMA

> From the Wendy House to the National Theatre, humans seem to be able to illuminate significant truths about their condition by watching and taking part in enactments.

Even a cursory examination of our Western culture discovers the centrality of drama to our lives. Although we may not visit the theatre often, we cannot escape bombardment by messages and stories in dramatic form, especially from television, where an increasing proportion of output is devoted to fiction. The very ubiquity of the dramatic form makes it an often unseen influence in our lives. David Hornbrook acknowledges the importance of this phenomenon: 'Dramatised stories of all kinds pervade our lives, many standing as key metaphors through which we make sense of the world' (Hornbrook, 1991, p.63).

It is not just that these dramatized fictions form a retrospective commentary on our culture. By engaging with them we find symbolic ways of representing the elements that most concern us in our lives:

> Drama has become one of the principal means of communication of ideas and, even more importantly, modes of human behaviour in our civilisation: drama provides some of the principal role models by which individuals form their identity and ideals, set patterns of communal behaviour, form values and aspirations. (Willis, 1990, p.49)

If there is general acknowledgement of the power and place of drama in our culture, there is little agreement about drama's purpose in education, where a fierce debate has raged amongst the theorists. On one side stand those who give priority to drama's role in child development, on the other those who see drama as an art form indivisible from theatre. The former blame the latter for introducing alien theatrical approaches to activities which they feel should be unsullied by notions of performance and audience.

> Children ... leave us with the responsibility of protecting them from the audience experience in order to retain and develop factors of far greater importance. (Way, 1967, p.14)

The latter blame the former's inability to align drama with the other arts for its exclusion as a discrete subject from the National Curriculum:

> The time has come for drama to reclaim its rightful artistic territory of theatre and text and to enter unequivocally into the generic community of the arts. (Peter Abbs in Hornbrook, 1991, preface)

The old schism has its roots in the days when drama first emerged as a distinct educational medium. In the 1930s and 1940s the term drama was virtually synonymous with theatre and as the mould-breakers did not want their work to be misunderstood, they held theatre at arm's length, giving their drama the prefix 'child', 'educational' or 'creative'.

Unlike the theorists, however, many drama practitioners now embrace both viewpoints. They see drama as a continuum. At one end lies improvisation, often unrepeated, where learning takes place through the very act of participating and reflecting, and at the other, full-blown theatre. They are confident in knowing on which part of the continuum they are operating and their work moves easily between the use of drama as hypothesis and drama as theatre. HMI also recognizes this spread of dramatic activity:

> Drama in schools is a practical artistic subject. It ranges from children's structured play, through classroom improvisations and performances of specially devised material to performances of Shakespeare. (HMI, 1989, p.1)

The extremes may appear obvious. The unselfconscious 'organized play' of the home corner in an infant classroom and the West End production can be assuredly placed, but within the extremities, the relationship of theatrical form to everyday drama teaching is a more complex affair.

Drama and the National Curriculum

There is a distinct difference between the place envisaged for drama in the National Curriculum and the one it currently holds in many schools, where inspired teaching and the mounting of relevant productions can make it a valued and high-profile component of a 'broad and balanced curriculum'. Yet there is strong support for the idea that drama should be seen as both a teaching method and a coherent specialism: 'While drama is recognised in the National Curriculum as an invaluable teaching method, it is first and foremost an art form in its own right' (ACGB, 1992, p.i).

My contention is that drama should remain a discrete subject with its own agenda whilst capitalizing on its role in relation to other subjects, as suggested in the National Curriculum. This book attempts to elevate and make more central the role of drama in relation to other subjects, both in the day-to-day liaison between teachers of drama and other subject specialists who may see drama as an ideal way to enhance the teaching of their own specialism, and as a catalyst and focus in major curriculum projects which may culminate in performance.

The place of skills

If students are to be successful in representing their ideas in drama, they must acquire, at appropriate times in their personal and dramatic development, the skills that will enable them to control and manipulate the medium. Some of the major skills are dealt with in Chapter 3. Teachers must beware of being too concerned with skill acquisition – infants using a classroom activity area would not benefit from an intensive session on mime, for instance – but should be ready to promote conscious consideration of new skills or the extension of existing ones when it is clear their students' work would benefit.

Drama as art form

There is a growing understanding amongst teachers that students must become aware of the aesthetics of the medium. Its realized form stands alongside those of the other arts, and severe limitations will arise where teachers fail to exploit its potential. Development of students' aesthetic sense will be aided by skills teaching and an understanding of theatre forms and content.

Improvisation

The distinctive feature of most drama is improvisation, or 'acting out', as the Schools' Council Drama Teaching Project preferred to call it. This involves students 'making an imaginative leap from their actual situation or roles into a supposed one' (McGregor *et al.*, 1977, p.11), allowing them to enter a role 'as if' they were that person. The safety of knowing they are not, and can withdraw from the situation should they wish to, allows them to enter more fully into the drama, experimenting with attitudes and reactions different from their own. In role, the students enter into what Ken Byron calls a 'shared fiction' or 'an agreement to pretend' (Byron, 1986, p.22).

The students' ability to differentiate between the real and the symbolic allows them to enter into the drama without fear of the consequences that might result from such a situation in real life. Their sense of 'outness' or detachment also enables them to view the model critically and to rerun it having changed some variables:

> Let's try it again where the rains *do* come.
> This time, the leader is less sure of the facts.

Drama also allows pupils to speak from a kind of firsthand experience. Instead of '*they* might feel angry that the daughter didn't tell the exact truth about the night before', pupils say '*I* couldn't tell them. *I* intended to, but when *I* looked at their faces, *I* knew it would start a row, so *I* took the easy way out.'

The relationship that exists between the imagined and the real is the key to the learning process unique to drama. Augusto Boal (1979) calls this state 'metaxis', a state of consciousness which holds the two forms in mind at the same time. Whilst engaging with the situation in the shoes of another, the student views what happens to the character from the reality of self. These double reference points in juxtaposition create the conditions where real, preconceived values and attitudes are placed in creative tension with those emerging in the scene being played. This appreciation of the difference between the individual's real opinions and those of the character being played is achieved within the drama: 'in a way that is often difficult to manage in everyday life, when our own reactions and feelings may be spontaneous' (HMI, 1989, p.1).

As already suggested, this state is normally easily achievable with very young students used to engaging in play, but teachers must decide what focus this structured play will have and decide how their intervention will aid it:

> In the early years, drama develops from creative and imaginative play. Teacher intervention in such activity is crucial if the children are to be helped to focus on learning objectives. (Rattray and Jones, 1991, p.1)

As the student progresses, a more conscious use of the medium is employed. Skills teaching is based on the maxim that to respect a medium, students must be able to control it.

In all this we must also remember the plethora of dramatic representations to which our students have access. The films and plays of BBC, ITV and the satellite stations, augmented by videos and the occasional radio play or visit to a theatre or cinema create a situation where 'The child of today can see more drama in a week than his or her great grand parents would have witnessed in a lifetime' (ACGB, 1990, p.10). Students consequently have access to a vast library of dramatic representation and the use of drama's symbolism to stand for the real world is, for most, an everyday experience, a phenomenon deeply embedded in our culture. The willingness of drama teachers to employ their expertise in the use of this language and make their subject relevant to the rest of the curriculum may be a crucial factor in the survival of the subject. This does not mean abandoning previous aims; it simply means a willingness to end the isolation which many teachers of drama court. They may have a better chance of convincing decision-makers of the value of their subject if that value is apparent to the generality of other specialists.

From sharing to performance

Once we move beyond the notion that *all* learning in drama is best acquired through engagement in unrepeated improvisations, students must learn to shape their symbolic dramatic representations to create more effective metaphors of their emerging understandings. These understandings are modified in the very attempt to capture them in the drama, and it is the productive tension between what we wish to say and the struggle to represent it which further energizes much of the drama process.

In the secondary phase and the later stages of the primary phase, once students have reached a kind of equilibrium where what they finally aspire to express in the drama matches their best attempt to do so, carefully articulated statements may have been created that could be shared with others to the mutual benefit of participants and audience (used in its widest sense of observers, appreciators). This audience might be classmates, members of other classes or schools, parents or the general public, and the sharing space could range from an informal cluster on the hall floor to a major performance venue. Teachers are now more adept at seeing even very ambitious and sophisticated performance as part of the seamless robe of drama. The cross-curricular case study described in Chapter 10 shows how such activity can be firmly rooted in drama's educational practices.

The eclectic nature of drama sources

Drama draws its material from the full range of human experience, and its approaches may be used to consider such sociological topics as poverty, family or old age, historical issues, concepts such as friendship and loyalty, story embedded in literature and just about anything that has human behaviour as its focus. The only imperative is that the conflict or tension which will energize the drama is clearly identified within the material and captured in the drama.

Drama as a focus for integrated learning

Although the curriculum is now conceived in its component parts, represented by the separate ring binders issued by the Department for Education, teachers must surely see the parts as contributing to a web of understanding about our world. Students should be able to see the relationship between gobbets of information gained in different areas of their lives and marshal them in synthesis. Drama has the ability to pull together disparate facets of learning, acting as an effective catalyst for the integration of this often compartmentalized knowledge. Its very eclecticism allows it to embrace the concerns of many other areas of students' educational experience.

Drama as an opportunity to live through the human implications of knowledge

> Events are enacted or unfold before our eyes. So it is a powerful way of bringing alive knowledge and experience which might otherwise be inert. (HMI, 1989, p.7)

Every good teacher will know the limitations of discussing topics through generalizations. The history teacher who asks pupils what it was like to have lived in the days of the Black Death will soon meet the responses –

- It would depend where you lived.
- It would depend on whether or not you caught it.
- Would you have had money to survive the death of the breadwinner?

In order to make worthwhile judgements about how people might respond in particular settings, participants need to know the detail of the circumstances in which decisions would be made and action taken. Drama allows us to invent or research the detail of human circumstance, so that the actions of participants can be informed by many of the factors that might be taken into account in real life.

A simple and often-used example might be a discussion about the reaction of a parent to a teenage son or daughter who had promised to be in by midnight and who is seen being dropped off by car outside the house at three in the morning. The course of events at breakfast next morning would depend upon factors such as the following:

13

- Is this the first time the teenager has arrived home late?
- Where had she been – to a rave or to a school reunion?
- Was the car a police car or that of a trusted friend?
- Was the lateness unavoidable, or was it due to a direct flouting of the agreements reached between teenager and parent?

It is clear that this contextual information will affect the way in which the participants react. The course of events will be further influenced by the personalities of the individuals involved and the relationship between them. If the parent is an unreasonable person with a quick temper, the outcome will almost certainly differ from that occurring if he had been reasonable and calm.

Such information would have to be taken into account if drama was used to explore this kind of situation. Some of it can be given by the teacher, some devised by the students before the improvisation starts, and yet more invented by the participants as the improvisation progresses. When a detailed dramatic model has been achieved, students are making decisions within a realistic representation of human behaviour.

In the course of primary school humanities, the teacher may wish to look at the issue of poverty in the Third World. Unless the topic is to be dealt with simply in statistical terms, the detail of human circumstances must be created to see how poverty affects individuals and families. We cannot for long, especially within this age-group, deal with poverty as an abstract generalization. I am not suggesting that useful work cannot be done without using drama approaches, simply that drama can be a powerful tool in allowing students to experience the 'feeling' aspects of the condition, to achieve empathy. Nor is the learning restricted to 'feelings'. It is reasonable to assume that factual material at students' disposal will inform their drama work, and that they will gain from seeing these factual understandings in a human context. Knowing how far Ethiopian women have to walk to collect firewood, the staple diet of the group they are studying or the worsening climatic conditions of the area will obviously be of use in arriving at a drama model which has integrity and relevance. It is one of the curses of poor drama that it is not informed by enough understanding of the background issues that condition behaviour and decisions. Although the students can never experience the awfulness of Third World hunger, carefully constructed drama, which avoids cliché, can enable them to begin to feel and understand that state.

Drama therefore can provide a powerful learning experience. Its power is rooted in the moral, social and aesthetic concerns and judgements of individuals, played out in the real social network of the drama group. For this process to function effectively, students need access to the basic skills of the medium.

Chapter 3
SKILLS

Effective use of an art form requires the mastery of skills. To make music at more than a very elementary level, students need to control the interpretative potential of instruments, whilst in fine art the command of materials and techniques must grow if developing artists are to retain confidence in their ability to employ the medium effectively. As the chief expressive mediums in drama are the body and voice, often used in entirely naturalistic ways, the skills can be less obvious, but their identification and acquisition are just as important here as in other art forms. Gavin Bolton, one of our foremost drama theoreticians, and sometimes considered hostile to the conscious acquisition of dramatic skills, does acknowledge their place, and supports:

> the teaching (often indirect) of dramatic form – at a level more fundamental than acting techniques, a level that dissolves the rigid distinctions drawn in the past between drama and theatre by harnessing what they have in common. (Nixon, 1982, p.42)

Proficient use of dramatic form requires the command of a symbolic language which stands for the real world. Those engaged in drama use voice, gesture, body form, costume, colour, light and sound to symbolize life's events. When we are making drama we are negotiating the form and meaning of these symbols at a real level – through reflective discussion, explanation and adaptation of the action – and from within the drama as we actually engage with it. Symbolic representations exist in the drama we create ourselves and in that which we witness as audience. When we are engaged with them, we constantly attempt to invest them with meaning, to make them intelligible in relation to our own biography. When this happens, 'elements of this internalised sensibility (of our culture) suddenly coincide with their representations in the culture itself and burst vividly into our consciousness' (Hornbrook, 1991, p.37).

The skills which allow us to create these representations are acquired, consciously or not, wherever drama is experienced. In our current education system, this process accelerates in the early years of secondary schooling. Teachers of drama must develop a skills teaching

16

framework which is appropriate to the age-groups they teach and extends the students progressively. The following are the main skills students need if they are to handle the dramatic medium with confidence.

Human skills

Improvisation – the central skill

Improvisation is a drama technique used to explore the human condition. It models real life situations, allowing participants to gain an experience close to the one being studied whilst appreciating that they are not involved in the real thing.

Before erecting a suspension bridge, engineers would build a scale model and subject it to equivalent strains and stresses to those expected for the real thing. The reality of the bridge will be informed by the results of the modelling. Similarly, drama creates paradigms of life in which variables can be changed and added, allowing participants to enter into and reflect upon dynamic human situations.

As the bridge model would be of little use if it were not used to explore the real structure's behaviour in the extreme conditions of use, so the improvisation has to focus on the problems inherent in the situation being examined. It is this which fuels the drama work and decisions in this area are some of the most crucial to be made by the teacher of drama. The following example may help in considering this point.

If an improvisation is set up where a middle-aged son visits an elderly mother each Sunday, always finding her in good health and circumstances, we do not have the requirements for productive drama. However, if the son's visits are in his lunch hour and, once at his mother's, he has to prepare hot food for her midday meal before rushing back to work, and if he detects signs that his mother is increasingly incapable of looking after herself, confirmed by a letter from the home help who is also worried, then we have the stuff of drama – tension.

For the bridge model to be of use, a number of variables would have to be set – the width of the span; the size of the cables; expected wind speeds; loads carried. In the same way, the improvisation needs to be informed by information about who the characters are; the physical surroundings; the time of day; the starting and sometimes the ending point of the improvisation; time-span and special information. Elements of this information can be, and often are, provided by the teacher, but some will be decided by the pupils.

17

The characters

It is a moot point as to how much we can ever 'be somebody else' within the drama. To a great extent we are always reacting as ourselves. Even when we are apparently fully engaged with a role, it seems certain that our ability to be both in and out of the experience is an essential ingredient of the learning that takes place.

If we are to take on a role which differs from our real self, we need to define the nature of that character. The teacher can do this by verbal description if the details are not extensive, or by role card if they are. The directions will include straightforward information such as age, occupation, social standing, likes and dislikes and attitudes to others in the scene. They will also contain more subtle signals embedded in information which is not so straightforward – previous experience of the problem being explored; particular aspirations held; indications of a disappointment experienced, for instance. Before characters are brought together in scenes, it is important that participants are given sufficient time to develop a solidity of characterization which can be sustained within the improvisation. Advice on developing a character is given later in this chapter.

The physical surroundings

One skill which pupils will need to acquire early on is the ability to create the different environments in which the dramas take place. Sometimes this can be achieved with the use of the materials available to them – rostra, tables and chairs and lengths of material, for instance.

> *Use the chairs, blocks and tubes to build the room which contains the astral telescope.*

These will often be augmented or completely replaced by surroundings created entirely within the imagination.

> *You are going to be in a cave about four metres by six. Decide what the floor is like; whether the walls are smooth or rough; where and how big the entrance is; how much natural light enters.*

Owing to the size of the class, it is likely that group areas will overlap. It never ceases to amaze me how 35 pupils in seven separate groups can concentrate on their own particular drama whilst surrounded by the often essentially noisy presence of others. The teacher must encourage concentration, protect the right of each group to remain undisturbed in its working space and ensure that resources are distributed fairly. The resentment caused by one group grabbing all the rostra, for instance, can be corrosive.

The time of day

This may seem an insignificant point, but it isn't. It *matters* when a scene takes place. If a daughter wishes to tell her mother that she has decided to leave home, whether the scene takes place at 8 a.m. while the working mother is gobbling the last of her breakfast or in the evening when there is plenty of time to discuss matters can have a crucial effect on the way the improvisation develops. Often the time fix given will be accompanied by other contextual information:

> *It's 7 p.m., and at this time you always like to go to your bedroom to be alone for a while and play music.*

> *It's 7 a.m., and as you look out of the bedroom window you see that your neighbour has again parked in front of your garage doors.*

The starting point

Making a clean start to the improvisation is essential. Exact information on what characters are doing as it begins should be given.

> *Get into a still position. David is putting the box back into its hiding place under the floorboard and the two police officers are about to knock on the door.*

The starting point often ensures that characters are positioned in relation to each other in ways which will lock them on to the problem to be explored.

> *As A prepares to climb back over B's fence, B emerges from her back door with the remains of the broken gnome in her hands.*

> *The manager is pinning up the list of compulsory redundancies as the employee calls by to collect the 'Best Salesperson of the Month' award.*

Failure to find a suitable juxtaposition can lead to an improvisation taking an inordinate time to reach the focus, going off at half-cock or at a tangent.

19

Time-span and end-point

There are times when the teacher wants all of the improvisations to end at or around the same time. Students should be given an indication of the length of the work:

This improvisation will take about five minutes.

Students become quite skilled in fitting their work to an approximate time-span, especially if they are aided by indications of time passing. This can be achieved by the teacher raising an arm when there is one minute left, by the use of a cardboard clock, or by the teacher calling out when there is one minute, then half a minute, left.

Sometimes an end-point is given:

The improvisation ends when
– the mother leaves for work;
– the girls find the box;
– Michael realizes he has been cheated;
– the shopkeeper says, 'You bring it back and I'll have a look, but I can't promise, mind you.'

Not all groups will finish at the same time. This can be because groups are exploring a scene in an open-ended way or, having been given a time-span for the work, finish a little behind or ahead of others. It is imperative that groups which have finished do not disturb those still working. Suitable instructions may be:

When you have finished
– sit quietly in your space until everyone has finished;
– sit on the floor together and talk quietly about how the explorers coped;
– come and sit by me;
– come and collect the paper and pens on which you will list the demands made by the Queen.

The teacher should be able to recognize the point at which all improvisations have been completed. Asking students to sit or behave in particular ways aids teacher judgement on this.

Special information

In some improvisations it is essential that only particular characters possess certain information. In an improvisation about A's desperate attempts to get back a beloved object loaned against better judgement to B, only B may be told that the object is broken and this is why it has not been returned earlier. American Indians who challenge settlers opening a mine may be told that this is a sacred site for their tribe, whilst the settlers remain in ignorance of this. The special information energizes the exploration of the issue being examined in a way that general disclosure of such material would not.

In summary, before starting most improvisations, students need to know:

- who they are (the characters);
- where they are (the physical surroundings);
- the time of day;
- the starting point;
- the time-span and end-point;
- special information.

Jamming

Participants should respond in ways which allow the improvisation to grow. Initially, some can derive satisfaction from frustrating their partners' attempts to develop a coherent progression – jamming – and this can result in a haphazard structure with little focus. Such behaviour should be discouraged gently but firmly as once its pleasures have been tasted, it can begin to be seen by students as the 'clever person's response'. Co-operative attitudes are vital to successful drama.

Explaining improvisation to pupils

It is useful if pupils have some conception of how improvisation works. I usually explain this with the use of a number of white plastic mugs of the kind used in drinks dispensers, although coloured cubes or other suitable objects would do as well. Stick different coloured shapes to the sides of the mugs to give them individual identity and position them in two groups to represent the ideas two participants bring to an improvisation. Place one mug in clear space to show how one person within the improvisation starts it off. Explain how, after absorbing the other's contribution, the second person adds an idea to the first. Continue to build a physical structure with the ideas/mugs to represent the developing improvisation. When it is complete, stress that no such work has *ever* existed in that exact form before and this represents the uniqueness of the product of the art form. You can demonstrate the need for a high level of co-operation between the two participants by showing that a refusal to co-operate can result in two unrelated structures or, where the intention of one of the participants

is destructive, the demolition of the whole structure. This representation is not an exact match of the drama process, but I have found it
most useful in giving participants a simple understanding which can
be referred to at appropriate moments within drama activity.

Role playing and developing character

Many documents, including those that enshrine the National Curriculum, use the term 'role play' instead of 'improvisation' or 'acting out'.
Drama teachers usually understand role play as the playing of a role
which represents a set of attitudes or values. It draws on our
knowledge of stereotypes and archetypes – the traffic warden, irate
motorist, obdurate shopkeeper and complaining customer – which can
quickly be identified with, adopted and played. The creation of the
personality and complexities of an individual is commonly referred to
as characterization, and takes much longer to develop. Matters are
confused a little by referring to someone who adopts a character as
being 'in role'.

There are many ways of approaching the adoption of character. In
general, characters cannot be found in isolation from the settings in
which they operate, so plenty of experience of *being* a character in
situations where characteristics can develop is the chief requirement.
Post-scene discussion on the way the character is developing can be
used to modify or change characteristics that have emerged:

> *I don't think she's as upset as that when she finds out. She's been
> expecting it, so she is almost relieved.*

> *I think I resent your presence more. I seemed to let you trample all
> over me that time – let's try it again where I'm much stronger in my
> response when you walk in.*

In playing a character, students can find it difficult to move very far
from their own personas. Exercises which enable them to make quite
radical shifts in physical, vocal and mental states are useful in
establishing what is possible. I have found the following exercise
useful in accomplishing this.

I once wanted some quite young students to adopt the characters of
old people. I knew that their portrayals would either make little
concession to the ageing process – very quick movements; their usual
voices – or succumb to the cliché of doddery movements with walking
sticks and high-pitched voices. To avoid this, I confronted them with
those clichés and told them we were to go through a process which
would lead to a more sincere portrayal.

We talked generally about old people they knew, and about some common characteristics of the age-group. We then talked about the individuality of old people and established the fact that they had all at one time been young. The latter helped create the notion of the child within old age, giving them a conceptual basis for their own youthful presence in the character's portrayal. Having spread the class out and asked each student to sit on a chair, I blindfolded them, thereby cutting out visual signals, which might undermine concentration on the task. I then did a talk-through which lasted around twenty minutes, focusing their attention on certain kinds of old people. I asked them to decide what kind of chair they were sitting in and what furniture surrounded them – the carpet, chairside table, sideboard and magazine rack, for example. I asked them to run their 'inner eye' around the room, looking at the space in detail – pictures and photographs, mementoes, other objects. I asked them to work out the physical feel of sitting in the chair and to adjust their bodies to suit. I followed this with talk-through on their breathing and how they felt about this room and being in it. I gave them a number of possible states – were they content, and expecting a visitor soon, or fed-up and lonely, for instance.

Having established the mental state, I asked them to get up out of the chair and to move around it to pick up something before sitting down again. In this part of the exercise, they discovered more about their physical selves – how they walked; how easy or difficult it was to get in and out of the chair; their strength. Continuing with the talk-through, I asked them to create the wider environment – family, friends, neighbours, tradespeople who might call; how they get their shopping; how long they have lived in this house. Having reinforced their physical nature through an attempt to find an object on a nearby table, I asked them to speak an internal monologue on how they are feeling today and what they are thinking about. I gave them a couple of minutes to feel what their state of mind was and then counted to three, at which point they all started talking at the same time, thereby avoiding the potential embarrassment of being the first to speak. The voices were amazing, forged from all the previous work on the character, especially the body posture elements, and avoiding the clichéd response mentioned earlier. After the monologue, I asked all to sit down again before helping individuals from their space into that of another student, guiding them – still blindfolded – and sitting them down next to the other character. As I delivered individuals to a partner I simply asked them to talk to one another, and this they did without embarrassment. As, in this particular class, the different sexes had found difficulty in working together, boys worked with girls if I could arrange it. After about ten minutes of conversation, I asked them to commit the characters to their physical and emotional memories before I talked them out of it. When I asked them to remove the blindfold, most had no idea which student in role they had been talking to. The work of subsequent lessons benefited from the establishment of such strong characters, and although I did not use the blindfold technique again with those students, I was able to refer to that exercise and the feelings it generated whenever I wished them to get into other characters. It set a quality threshold and gave them an experience of how satisfying a properly developed character could be.

Naturalistic and stylized forms

Much drama is a 'slice of life'. Its action mimics the speech and movement of our real lives and takes place in 'real' locations. Students have little difficulty in mastering this side of things, and for younger children it is so similar to the world of play they so often inhabit that they find a ready home within it.

Stylization uses symbols which represent reality without faithfully mirroring it. Often it compresses meaning and allows a much more economic form of expression. Notions of naturalistic and stylized form are easily nurtured, even in quite young students. Short naturalistic pieces can be stylized as a way of introducing the concept. This can be achieved through the use of movement and mime – a real argument being represented by physical threat and counter-threat in stylized movement, for instance; a distillation of language – key phrases or words taken from a naturalistic scene spoken chorally whilst the characters represent the progress of the scene in a number of tableaux; songs – which describe a battle as the conflict is conducted in mime; narration – by one character of her inner feelings for another while she circles the unhearing subject of her comment; poems – devised and spoken to a movement piece which itself is derived from an earlier naturalistic scene, and often a combination of such techniques.

At a more sophisticated level, whole naturalistic dramas can be stylized. A *naturalistic* piece on conditions for child workers in the cotton mills of the early nineteenth century might include the following scenes:

1   Girl worker in family scene. Bread and scrape breakfast at 5 a.m.
2   Girl on way to work with fellow workers. They are ambushed by aggressive boy workers.

3 At work on the machines. As a punishment and an example to the other young workers, the overseer suspends a sleepy young boy by his ankles in a cold-water butt.
4 In an attempt to work harder, the young girl gets her hand caught in a machine and is badly injured.
5 Girl in bed at home, surrounded by family. Her mother comforts her.

In *stylized* form this might become:
Mother and daughter sit on stools either side of the acting area, facing front, not each other. The daughter has one arm in a bloody sling. A number of other students form a group between and behind these stools. The characters speak snatches of dialogue from the naturalistic scenes. Everyone directs their words to the front. Because the daughter is already injured, it is clear that all the scenes are flashbacks.

1 Injured girl's narration interspersed with short pieces of dialogue from the naturalistic scene. These may not all be spoken by those who originally did so.
2 Girl walks on spot in front of stool, narrating. Group become the boys hiding. They represent the threat posed to the girl by gradually closing on her. At a given point they leap forward with a shout, holding a tableau of nightmarish poses.
3 As girl describes the boy being held in the water, group represents thrashing water sounds and the voices of overseer and boy.
4 As girl tells of working harder, group becomes menace of machinery in sound and movement. This reaches a climax with a single scream as the machine closes on its victim and a bloodstained hand is thrust above it.
5 Almost complete stillness and quiet as a contrast to the end of scene 4. The daughter narrates how the family responded. This is interspersed with words from the mother on her stool and other family members who emerge from the group.

Once students have a confident understanding of these two major forms of drama, their dramatic vocabulary is extended in a most productive way. Ability to switch between the two, or to use them in combination, greatly enriches their work.

Mime

Mime is a classic stylized form. It enables participants to explore or communicate the essence of a situation without the clutter of real time, settings or characterization. Children take readily to it and quickly master its use. There is usually little point in systematically teaching the detailed skills contained in mime courses and books. Fixed point, the technique which allows a mime to keep her trapped hand fixed in the mouth of an imaginary letterbox whilst she struggles to remove it, can be an interesting skill for students to learn, but it and others like it are best dropped into the repertoire of individuals or groups at appropriate moments of need.

The chief purpose of mime skills is to free students from the actuality of physical surroundings. Most of the time, usually intentionally, we do not have the furniture and hand props required, so they must be imagined. Mimed objects are often preferable to the real thing. We can imagine a much more splendid crown than any which is likely to be available, and miming the fish tank that is dropped as its new owner carries it from the shop has obvious advantages over using an actual tank! Children can become distracted from the most important job in hand – the development of human dramatic potential – by an often lengthy and not always successful search for the correct objects and costumes. Once one real object is introduced, the convention can demand that others in that scene must be sought too. Perhaps the greatest advantage of imagined physical surroundings is that they can be changed instantly at will. Changing an imaginary sword into an imaginary club does not entail an often fruitless search in the drama cupboard.

One way to introduce a sense of mime is to concentrate for a period on the mime skills students use naturally within their general drama:

> *Let's see if we can really get the sense of these heavy boxes you are loading on to the ship.*

> *Remember, you are digging the tunnel with a spade that's very hard to use in such a small space, and all the soil must be passed back in buckets that have been filled by hand.*

This sort of guidance should lead to a sharper and more satisfying representation without making the students overly conscious of the mime to the detriment of other, more central aspects of the drama.

Another simple way of introducing mime is to show an appropriate videotaped episode which relies principally on language for effect, with the sound turned off. Ask the students what they think it's about, then play it again with sound. Discuss what modifications would be needed if this episode were to be devoid of words. What would they need to do to the action to compensate? After inventing such a scene in mime, apply the approach to some of their own work.

If the Queen can't speak when she inspects her subjects to find someone who can make her laugh, what would happen to the action?

Several straightforward techniques and guide-lines can help:

1 The mimed physical environment should be respected by all within the drama. If a wall with a worktop has been established, it can be disconcerting and disruptive to have an individual walk through it!
2 The weight and size of objects should be considered. This relates to:
3 The body balance and effort that go into the use of objects, for example a sledgehammer or a typewriter.
4 Groups should have a shared understanding of the physical environment – how high is the window-ledge? Is it a sash or a hinged casement? Does the door have a knob or a catch? This cannot and should not be discussed in great detail before running the drama. Most of the consensus comes from careful observation of the work in progress, but exercises like the one where a pair shift a large sheet of glass together, carry it to another place and put it down can help in fostering the close observation and co-operation required.
5 Actions must be exact. Poor mime, for example, will often result in a full mug of hot tea being lifted quickly and tipped at 45 degrees well before it reaches the lips.
6 Attention must be paid to the focus of the eyes. A person watches a full mug carefully as they lift it; someone fitting a small key into a door lock looks at the target intently.
7 Mime often works best when movements are relatively isolated. In that it is representative of the real thing, even 'naturalistic' mime may be adapted to allow it to do its job with more clarity. The maxim is: 'One move at a time.'
8 Perhaps the one specialist technique worth teaching is the 'snap-on/snap-off'. This is a simple signal to show when the hand comes into and out of contact with an object. In the snap-on, it helps to imagine the hand and the object as unlike magnetic poles. When the hand is an inch or two from the object, it suddenly closes on it, taking up an appropriate shape. With the snap-off, think of the hand and object as becoming like poles: the hand springs a little from the object as it loses touch with it. This sounds terribly false, but it is very effective in giving form to mimed detail, and students quickly get the hang of it.

It helps to think of mime in three contexts; the *naturalistic* form described above, where it usually accompanies speech; more *stylized* mime where the world is represented through action, often without words; and *fantasy* mime, where the normal rules of the world are bent to allow the fantastic to happen. Students shrink themselves and eat their way into an apple, carve the pip into a sculpture or help a grub bore its hole, or compress the giant's castle to the size of an Oxo cube and pop it into their mouths.

Over-promotion of mime to the detriment of other skills can give rise to hollow and destructively self-conscious work. Used judiciously, however, it can become an indispensable part of the dramatic vocabulary.

Movement

I use the term 'movement' to differentiate between the less formal approaches described here and the more organized and technique-based forms of dance. In practice the two may overlap productively.

Students, especially young ones, use expressive movement quite naturally. This characteristic disappears for most at the onset of adulthood, and from then on movement which deviates from accepted functional form is usually found only within adult play and game structures – the disco, sports field and beach, for example. It is important to bring movement into the drama not only to widen the dramatic skill base, but also to enable students to be in touch with their physical, emotional and expressive selves in ways that may be liberating and help them develop.

Movement of the 'put on a record and move as the music suggests' kind held sway in the 1960s, when the liberation of the inner, creative self through the process was deemed to be of paramount importance. Work of the 1970s and early 1980s was more technique- and product-based and the disciplined medium of dance strengthened its presence. The last few years have seen the emergence of a 'midway' model, a balance between the two.

With young students, it is unnecessary and inhibiting to make them overly aware of their movement. They partake of physical experiment-ation and repetition naturally within their games, and in the freedom of the park, garden or playground, they hop, skip, jump and twirl as the mood demands. Very young children are especially affected by rhythmic sound, and it is at this less conscious level that infant and lower junior movement should operate. Even here, however, teacher intervention is required to give structure to the form and develop movement skills. Improvisation is important, but students will often need to select, phrase and refine the movement that flows from it.

Gradually, as more control is required, a greater awareness of what their bodies can achieve in both exploration and communication phases can be introduced. Basic techniques developed by movement pioneer Rudolph Laban (Preston, 1963) can be used to give a framework for developing a movement vocabulary and I have freely adapted some of his approaches in my work with students of all ages. The following section includes only those elements I have found most useful, and in no way amounts to a comprehensive explanation of Laban technique. Teachers wishing to know more should consult the Further Reading section.

How the body moves

Time See this as a continuum covering the length of time a movement takes. At one end is *sudden* movement, at the other *sustained*. These movement qualities can be practised to percussion sounds and put together in sequences – a sustained, followed by three sudden and a sustained, for example. A tremendous sense of excitement and anticipation can be generated in this work. At first, sequences can be developed by individuals, but progress to paired and group sequences can be rapid.

Weight At one end of the continuum is *strong* movement, at the other, *light*. Strong movement involves muscle tension, light more relaxed and deft movement. Use percussion sound to develop and sequence these qualities. Once they are understood and a degree of control is evident, this continuum can be permutated with the time scale – sudden strong movements, sustained light. Combinations of time and weight give movements a sense of rhythm.

Where the body moves

Space This is the area in which the body moves. Personal space surrounds the individual, and conceptually its shape resembles a large, traditional domed beehive. Common space refers to all space other than the spaces occupied by students, and individuals can make journeys through it without encroaching on each other's personal space. Spaces can be explored using movement qualities already covered: explore your personal space using strong sustained movement.

A useful way of establishing a sense of personal space is to ask students to curl up small as though shrink-wrapped in plastic. Keeping at all times a part of their body in contact with the spot on the floor where they curled up, ask them to use their expanding body to push away the plastic all around them until they can reach no further. The 'beehive' shape results. Interesting exercises can be introduced using personal space – the touching spaces of two individuals can be explored, invaded, colonized, shared, the whole encounter being conducted in movement, for example. With a large class properly spaced out, the relative positioning of personal and common spaces can be grasped by asking the students to imagine a similar number of large inverted drinking-glasses pushed tightly against each other on a shelf. The glass rims represent the perimeter of their personal spaces, with the amoeba-like shapes in between as common space.

Levels This refers to how low or high the movement is. It can be split into low (nearest the floor), medium (thighs to shoulders) and high (shoulders to as high as you can jump). This quality can be permutated with others – low strong sustained; high sudden light movements.

Dimensions – spatial actions This is the direction of the movement when viewed from the originator's standpoint: up–down, right–left, forward–backward. The actions that relate to these directions are rising/falling, opening/crossing, advancing/retreating.

Diagonals Movements can follow a diagonal line. Imagine standing in a hollow cube with its corners at the extent of your reach. The lines run diagonally from corner to corner through the centre of the body as follows:

> high-right-forward to deep-left-backward
> high-left-forward to deep-right-backward
> high-left-backward to deep-right-forward
> high-right-backward to deep-left-forward

Dimensions and diagonals can be explored by individuals before making use of the movements in pairs and groups to create movement patterns based on known forms – symmetrical and asymmetrical shapes, for example.

The combination of the elements of time, weight and space in varying ways gives movement its *dynamics,* which is the word now used in place of Laban's term, *effort.* Dynamics give expression and 'colour' to movement.

With whom the body moves

Support positions When individuals work with others, they can hold positions that would be impossible on their own. One example is the pair facing each other, toes touching, holding hands. Using the other as a counterweight, each leans back until arms are straight and the position is stable. Another is a student supported on the back of another who is on all fours. Many different positions can be created, and students should be allowed to discover them. A useful extension can involve finding a sequence of moves into and out of the support position. The teacher can count eight into the position and then eight out. The counting could then be replaced by percussion sounds. At all times, the movement should be controlled and balanced.

Moving with others Key words to describe the qualities here are meeting and parting, approaching, clashing and merging. The latter two describe movement which is either in some kind of harmony, or in disharmony.

What the body does

Stillness In the same way that light is most effective in drama when contrasted with the lack of it, and sound works best when contrasted with silence, students should be encouraged to explore the relationship between movement and stillness. Stillness requires balance and muscle control and may be included at points within a movement sequence as well as at its start and end.

Jump There are five basic jumps: from one foot to the same foot, from one foot to the other, from one foot to both, from both feet to one, from both feet to both feet. Students can experiment with combinations and variations of these.

Travel Getting from one point to another using a variety of movements – running, walking, crawling, jumping and rolling are some of the possibilities. This quality links with the support positions mentioned above.

Turn This means changing the overall direction of travel. The turn can be led by different parts of the body – eyes, hand, leg, shoulder, head, back, elbow.

Gesture A movement of a limb or the body to express feelings. Gestures allow the body to speak without words.

Balance points The points of contact with the floor. The most obvious are feet and hands in combination, but experiment with others – knees, elbows, shoulders, buttocks, heads. This work can be developed by describing the body as 'modelling material' which does not always represent the human form. It can be moulded and placed in different positions on the floor.

Transference of weight Using balance points in combination, whilst transferring the body weight in a controlled movement sequence.

Other useful aspects

Neutral position A very important notion. Students stand legs slightly apart, arms at sides, spine extended, head held above body, eyes looking steadily forward. It is the 'nothing position', the equivalent of the ball of clay before modelling starts. Other neutral positions can be developed using different balance points.

Starting position This might be a neutral position or some other appropriate shape. The instructions 'Take a neutral position' or 'Find a starting position' precede most movement sequences.

Dress Students should be properly dressed for movement work. Loose clothing disguises and therefore blurs body shape. It is not necessary to advocate the widespread use of leotards and tights, although they can be worn if students wish. Track suits or stretch trousers and T-shirts are quite suitable. For sharing or performance, the students may wish to choose colours to match the mood of the piece they are developing. Symbolic appliqué can be glued or stitched to clothes for further effect.

Sound accompaniment I have spoken a lot about percussion. This need not be restricted to the usual drum and cymbal, but can embrace more unusual, esoteric and evocative sounds. The strings on an old piano frame can produce excellent variations of effect if struck with different kinds of beaters. Make use of other instrumental skills within the group. Flutes and cellos create the most wonderful atmospheres in which movement can take place and if you have access to an electronic keyboard consider its use too, though be careful that its potential volume and intricacies of effect do not swamp the movement.

Recorded sound There can be a temptation to use records, tapes or CDs for accompaniment. Take care here, for without re-recording and editing, the music can dominate the movement. Facilities for editing – reel-to-reel with an editing block or deck-to-deck if using cassettes –

can give students a sense of control. Students can compose and record music for their own movement and that of others.

A sample sequence

Starting points and content for movement can come from a variety of sources – music; poems; stories; pictures; real events; animal behaviour; abstract concepts. The following example, suitable for Year 5 and above, shows how the skills referred to above may be employed in combination and sequence.

Choose two contrasting concepts which will be effective in movement – jagged/smooth, suspicious/trusting, warlike/peaceable. Ask students to find a still position for each. Time should be given for experiment and the selection of a satisfying representation. Ask them to consider how one becomes the other – which part of the shape moves first, using what quality of movement, and does this quality change as they move towards the contrasting concept?

This can be further extended by building a sequence which has a number of fixed 'punctuation points': the life span of a person, idea, political movement or relationship, for instance. Students find starting and ending points, then four fixed, staged points in between. When these have been carefully chosen and crafted, they make them points in a continuous movement sequence. This could be simply lit, with beginning and end bracketed by blackout. The sequence might be accompanied by percussive or vocal sound – perhaps keywords or statements related to the content, carefully matched to the movement. Co-operation between groups can result in each creating live accompaniment for another.

Students should be introduced to aspects of this movement vocabulary only when the teacher feels they are ready to acquire additional expressive skills. Opportunities to practise and permutate movement qualities should be built into lessons on a regular basis.

Fights

Young people's drama often involves the portrayal of physical violence, especially at that age where story-making can centre on quasi-melodramatic situations and archetypes such as spies and robbers who are frequently involved in combat. Teacher-inspired work may also require the portrayal of violence, such as scenes from warfare. You may therefore wish students to acquire the ability to handle the representation of violence, in both naturalistic and stylized forms.

Fighting skills can be used in improvisation, but their main use is within constructed scenes.

There is a very real danger that pupils will become injured in uncontrolled fights. The real level of operation can intrude upon the symbolic – a boy playing the loser in a dramatized fight insists on winning because he feels he is, in real life, 'tougher' than the boy who is meant to beat him, for example. It is essential that we provide our pupils with the dramatic language to represent violence in ways that allow them to distance it from the 'real'. Some of the moves sound terrifying, but I have used them for many years without any student injury. Teachers should not enter into this kind of work lightly or for the thrills it can give. Lessons must be carefully planned and progress should be gentle, to allow proper acquisition and practice of the moves.

Naturalistic and stylized fights

Pupils will want to represent violence in a naturalistic form. They will have seen countless films and television programmes which employ the genre, so it is reasonable that they should be able to use it too. Unstructured naturalistic fights run the risk of either looking completely unconvincing – as when blows swing far from the opponent's body and there is no reaction to the 'punch' – or being so real that someone is injured. Pointing out this risk and offering to teach students the approaches which can bring conviction to this area of their work can be a useful starting point.

Whenever pupils are being asked to develop naturalistic fights, injury may result from unplanned blows and sudden contact with a hard floor. The latter can be mitigated by the use of agility mats. Some drama areas have ready access to these as the space may contain mats used in physical education lessons. Borrow some if they are available, or consider buying them specifically for drama use. In addition to their role as impact softeners, they provide a useful form of floor covering for young audiences. Injury as a result of unplanned blows can be obviated only by carefully planning and rehearsing the fight, starting with slow motion and building up to a more naturalistic speed.

Effective dramatic fights require mastery of the following moves and techniques:

Delivering punches Two main punches can be used – the punch to the head and the punch to the solar plexus. In each case it is important that both parties in the fight (and except in the rarest cases I would restrict the fight to two combatants) are aware of the sequence of moves and retain physical balance and stability. The best-aimed mock blow can cause damage if the receiver falls unbalanced into its path.

The head punch is best delivered by placing the non-punching hand on the victim's shoulder, as this physical link ensures greater accuracy in the move. The punch should be aimed 20 cm to the side of the head nearest the held shoulder and should end level with the ear to achieve maximum visual effect. The sound of the blow can be simulated by the assailant cupping, at the last moment, the hand holding the victim's shoulder and allowing the fist to smack into it. Alternatively the victim can slap hands together or strike his/her thigh, or an onlooker can produce sound similarly.

Head butts are delivered 25 cm away from the side of the victim's head. The assailant should place both hands on the victim's shoulders and both parties should be perfectly balanced before the move is carried out. Any audience should be placed to increase the apparent realism of the blow. The attacker's brow should stop a few centimetres 'into' the victim's head. Well-timed victim response is essential if this move is to be effective

The stomach punch should stop 10 cm short of the target's body, then gently follow the victim's physical response, to aid authenticity. The victim should be stationary during the delivery to ensure accuracy and should tighten the stomach muscles prior to the blow's delivery to provide some protection in the event of overshoot and contact.

Slaps can be very effective in a fight sequence. Care must be taken that fingernails do not rake the face or eyes. With a steadying hand on the victim's shoulder, the blow should usually be delivered with the other hand at least 10 cm in front of the face. To simulate the sound of the blow, the hand resting on the victim's shoulder should be brought in line with the striking hand at the last moment, allowing a realistic sound to be produced by contact of the two palms. Alternatively, the sound can be made by the victim or a watcher clapping hands at the appropriate moment.

Kicks should only be delivered to areas of the body which will not be damaged by unintentional follow-through. Like the stomach punch, they must stop 10 cm short of the victim's body, and be followed by a gentle contact with the victim's body to indicate when reaction should begin. The victim must be on the floor and quite still, to avoid injury. The toe of the attacking foot must be pointed down and the knee lead the action to present the flat surface of the top of the foot to the target.

The victim's body should be arched towards the striking foot to allow for a full physical reaction from the victim to the blow.

Knee in groin This should be delivered with the assailant placing both hands on the shoulders of the victim, while standing to one side with the striking knee next to the victim's body. The knee is brought straight up at least 15 cm outside the victim's thigh, taking care to end the blow level with it.

Hair pull The attacker clenches the fist and places it on top of the victim's head as though a handful of hair was being held. The victim uses both hands to hold the attacker's fist in place, one being placed on the attacker's wrist, the other on top of the fist. Authenticity is destroyed if the attacker's fist loses contact with the victim's head. If proper contact is maintained, the assailant can appear to wrench the victim about. Suitable noises in reaction to the supposed pain make this move effective and safe.

Holds These are best restricted to two: the head-lock and arm-lock. They are the stock-in-trade of professional wrestlers. In the head-lock, the attacker holds the victim's neck *loosely* near the hip. *Apparent* sudden tightening of the lock causes pain to the victim. It is essential that no actual pressure is applied to the neck. In fact no movement of the arm is necessary, as the effect is gained by the effort shown by the attacker and the simulated pain of the victim. The assailant must not pull the victim about and both parties must remain virtually stationary.

The arm-lock involves putting the victim's arm behind his back and, as with the head-lock, simulating sudden pressure on it. In fact there must be no movement of the arm and the victim's arm *must not be at the limit of its travel, to allow some safety margin.*

Rolls Two basic rolls should suffice: the buttock roll and the shoulder roll. The buttock roll is achieved by bending the knees while sitting down on the agility mat and bringing the legs over at an angle to do a *slanted* backward roll. Failure to slant this roll will lead to the body weight trapping the head and neck against the mat, with obvious dangers. The shoulder roll is a forward roll achieved by bending the knees, looking to one side, throwing the arm of the shoulder which will make contact with the mat to the side to which the head is looking, and then executing a slanted forward roll.

Falls The only one which is practical is the twist fall. This is achieved (say following a 'slap' to the face) by allowing the blow to turn the body and, when the back of the victim is turned to the assailant, falling forward on to the mat, breaking the fall with the hands. If preferred, the victim can go down on bended knees before falling fully on to the mat.

For these moves to be effective, they must be placed in the following contexts:

- There must be a convincing reason for the fight.
- The combatants must seem to want to hurt each other.
- There must be apparent effort and muscle tension in the blows.
- The effect of the blow, in both physical and vocal reaction, must be seen in the victim.

Given that these elements are present, and that any watchers are positioned so as to gain the maximum visual effect of the fight – on the side away from the delivered head punch and knee to the groin, for instance – the sequence can look very realistic.

It is recommended that the students start the fight sequence by working out the blow or move which ends the fight (end-blow) and then develop the sequence of moves leading up to that moment by working backwards, away from it to the start of the fight. This has the added advantage of imposing such a conscious development that the real level of aggression cannot flourish. All moves should be made in slow motion with a gradual build-up of pace. It is unlikely that the pupils will reach completely naturalistic speed in the early stages of learning these routines.

As the individual moves are added to the end-blow, the teacher should lead a controlled run through the growing sequence by counting the moves. It is recommended that no more than ten moves are used in the first instance.

Stylized fights can be conducted in slow motion and introduced into otherwise naturalistic drama. An example of this is where talks over a land dispute break down, and a battle breaks out between two rival groups. The stylized fights can be worked out in pairs beforehand, and as all pairs move at the same time, the effect is of a full-pitched battle. Stylized form allows combat to be represented in many forms – the combatants could be facing away from each other and be ten feet apart and still act and react in ways which link their actions into one fight. The battle might be in words – 'I cut to your shoulder', 'I parry your thrust to my chest', for instance, with the striking of metal to represent the clash of swords. Pupils can be very inventive, given the opportunity to develop alternatives to the naturalistic fight.

It cannot be stressed enough that this kind of work carries some risk, and it is the responsibility of teachers to make sure that all possible safety precautions are taken. This includes the removal of jewellery and normal footwear, the wearing of suitable clothing and sustained practice in slow motion. These are conscious skills which can greatly enhance the drama, but they must be taught with great care. Teachers of drama may wish to liaise with physical education specialists before attempting such sessions.

The work demands complete co-operation between partners, and balance and control are central to its success. In no circumstances should actual weapons or even replicas be used. Even a wooden sword can be dangerous if a fight goes wrong. Simple representations of weapons may be used in stylized fights as long as the teacher is convinced that no damage can occur.

Some of these moves may not be fully appropriate in the portrayal of fights between females. In my experience, it is a sad reflection on the male that girls have far less recourse to the portrayal of violence in their drama and, where they do, face slaps and hair pulling usually suffice.

The catalogue of instruction may seem horrific in the way it dispassionately describes such violent moves. I give the advice on the understanding that combat occurs in many forms of drama and the teacher should have strategies for its effective representation. It is essential that, having learnt these techniques, students do not seek every opportunity to include them in their drama. In my early attempts to teach drama, pupils showed a readiness to develop stories which always ended in a group bundle! Where pupils seem to descend too readily into dramatized violence, I would advocate an instruction which bans it completely from sections of the work.

Concentration

Drama's processes and products are often crafted with just as much deliberate skill as a painting or fine sculpture. Although many of the decisions are made outside the drama, there are moments of intense concentration within it when participants must be fully absorbed by the pull of the medium as they endeavour through improvisation to plumb the human condition they have chosen to explore. It is a major function of the teacher to create the conditions in which this can happen.

Technical skills

The above are human resource skills which are central to the making of effective drama. No amount of recorded sound, costume, lighting or other technical aid will compensate for their absence. Given their presence and continuing development, technical aids can enhance the drama experience. Early exploration of a topic is usually achieved without the need for such aids; they become more relevant when pupils are shaping their drama for possible sharing with others. At this level they help to enhance the meaning encapsulated within the drama. All electrical equipment, especially that to which students have access, should be tested regularly for safety.

Costume

Every teacher of drama knows the fruitlessness of the headlong dash for the costume box or cupboard and the encumbrance of ill-fitting or inappropriate items found there. Costumes should be used sparingly as they have massive potential to sidetrack the main objective of the lesson. It is a golden rule that we can often imagine a much better space suit, crown or cloak than that which is available in reality. If costume becomes too intrusive, students may come to think they cannot 'be' someone unless they have the correct clothes.

If these warnings are borne in mind, judicious use of simple pieces can heighten the drama experience. Lengths of coloured cloth and tabards and sashes can suffice. These can become cloaks, uniforms, or table and altar cloths, and the tabards can have symbols pinned to them to identify individual characters. Hats are usually the greatest block, as they rarely fit properly and can look absurd on small children.

Properties

These have the same limitations in use as costumes. Imaginary swords are wielded much more proficiently (and safely!) than the real thing, and crude wooden representations undermine the menace which such weapons often seek to represent. Use props sparingly and only when a decision has been taken by the students that the drama will be enhanced by them. As a general rule, exploratory drama has no need of them, but they will have their place as stimulus and at the communication stage.

Lighting

Most drama spaces now have blackout and at least simple lighting. Sometimes, especially in secondary schools, the lighting comprises the existing front of house spots, sited to light proscenium arch performances. Lanterns which are positioned on brackets mounted high on the wall or ceiling are usually incapable of being adjusted by pupils, not least because of safety fears or regulations. At best, schools now possess free-standing units which can be positioned within the drama space. These usually comprise lanterns on a T-bar and a dimmer

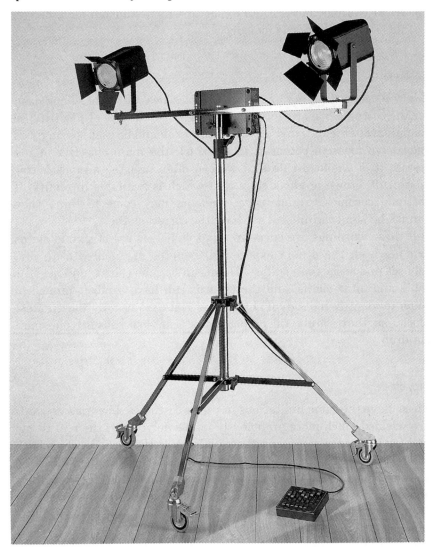

Figure 3.1 A free-standing lighting unit

control. They are ideal for group work and can be combined to provide adequate lighting for performances. Above all they are accessible to pupils, who can genuinely control their effect within their own drama. A suitable lighting unit, comprising two Minuette Fresnel lanterns, two barn-doors, a Mini Pack with a six-way control desk and a stand with locking castors is shown in Figure 3.1. It can be obtained from AJS Theatre Lighting & Stage Supplies Ltd., of Ringwood, Hampshire. The T-bar and dimming control will accept up to six lanterns, so schools with limited funding can add to the stock as money becomes available.

The greatest use of light should not be for effect through colour and atmosphere, but to help shape the drama by allowing images to fade in and out of blackout – an editing device. The 'life-span' sequence referred to earlier (see p.33) provides an example of how work can be enhanced by lighting. In blackout a single voice sings the melody of a song sung by mothers to babies. This is overlaid by a recording of a heartbeat. A single spot fades in gradually to reveal a 'baby' touching its face and sucking its thumb in turn, rhythmically. There is something magically powerful about crafted images appearing from and disappearing into darkness. It is one of the seminal experiences of drama.

In group-work different lighting conditions will be required in different parts of the space. It is very difficult to use sophisticated lighting during the exploration stage, as to achieve this for one group would almost certainly interfere with the work of others. It is wise to regulate the use of lights and to make them subservient to the human resources. The ideal is to acquire enough free-standing lighting units to allow each group control of its own area.

Rostra

These allow students to achieve different levels, creating a more interesting environment for drama activity. Different types include sophisticated folding rostra with castors, plastic or wooden blocks, tubular leg-frames and tops which can be built into different shapes and levels and a variety of folding wooden frames with multi-ply tops. Schools need to be sure their pupils can carry the blocks; constant sliding across the floor does the surface of neither much good, and rostra which are too heavy for students can cause damage to toes, fingers, walls and furniture. Some rostra fold neatly for storage, but rigid ones can take up a lot of space. The best rostra I ever used nested within one another, allowing six blocks to be stored in the space taken up by the largest.

41

Masks

Masks can be full- or half-face, the latter extending only down to the top lip, thus allowing unimpaired vocal sound. Examples of each type are shown in Figure 3.2. Basic ones can be made in cut-out card. These can be left simple, to be held in place by elastic, or the basic shape can be contoured by gluing on folded, curled or other shaped card. Detail and texture can be achieved by applying materials such as raffia, cloth and corrugated cardboard. The back of the head can be closed with fabric, allowing the mask to pull over the head. Hair can be attached to this fabric, if required.

Masks are often uncomfortable to wear as they pull too tightly against the eyes. This can be avoided if strips of foam are glued to the inside to rest on the forehead and cheeks.

More durable masks can be made from Celuflex, grade 55, available from Lee Chemicals Ltd., New Bridge Road, Glen Parva, Leicester LE2 9TD. This is torn into 3-cm squares, dipped into acetone and spread on to a face-shaped former to dry. Each square of material should be overlapped with the others and the edges blended in. Tearing rather than cutting helps in this blending as it gives a feathered edge. This is not a suitable material for widespread school use as stringent standards of ventilation and skin protection are necessary. It is excellent for the limited production of strong, well-defined masks. Strips of paper towel dipped into diluted PVA glue – 5 parts of water to 1 of glue – can be built up on a former, which can be made quite easily from clay. It is important that no underhangs are created which might impede the removal of the mask from its former. If this should happen, cut the mask in two and rejoin in the same material used for its manufacture. The surface of the former should be greased with petroleum jelly to aid removal of the completed mask. Allow the edges of the mask to extend beyond the expected facial boundary and trim them to shape when the mask is dry. This trimming and the nature and positioning of the eye-holes are crucial to the feel of the mask in use. Eye-hole positioning and size seem to dictate disproportionately the character which emerges. Tether the ends of strong elastic (not elastic bands) to the mask with staples, then cover the staples with further pieces of material. The mask should be subtly painted. Plain colours with a blushing of contrasting colour work well. Avoid bold complicated patterns, as these overpower the shape. Making and painting this kind of mask is an inexact science in that it is usually not possible to make a mask with a particular character in mind. Its true characteristics often only emerge in use.

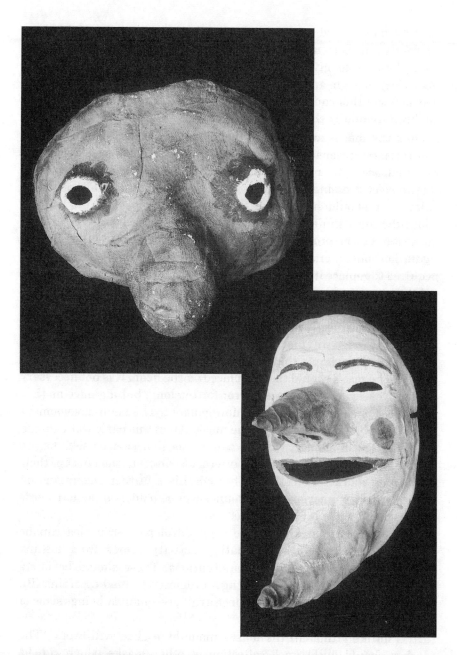

Figure 3.2 Completed full- and half-masks

Soft masks are made by pinning material around the head of the student before removing it for cutting to shape and gluing or sewing together. This kind of mask pulls on to the wearer's head and can be decorated or shaped by the fixing of additional materials. A 'skirt' can be fixed to the bottom edge of this and other kinds of masks and tucked into clothing to give complete coverage of head and neck. Many secondary design and technology departments will have a vacuum former, and this can be used to produce plastic masks. Students may make individually shaped formers from clay.

Once the masks are finished, they should be experimented with in workshop conditions with all students trying out all masks. Set up the drama space with a number of mirrors placed around the room. Old wardrobe or dressing-table mirrors are especially useful, although, for safety, you should ensure that they are properly backed and framed. Place the masks in a line on the floor to one side of the room. To aid characterization, provide a range of hats, coats and pieces of material, again laid out to one side. As students finish with an item, they are required to replace it where they found it.

Students should respect the process and the masks. If masks are worn and discarded too quickly, affect and effect will not have time to develop. After selecting a mask to try out, the student should look at it carefully to judge what feeling signals it gives off. This judgement need not be detailed: simply that the mask feels 'mean', 'timid', 'aggressive' or 'sly'. The mask should then be placed on the head. It is not necessary for the wearer to look into a mirror for too long, but a glance as they move past one can aid character development. The main development comes simply through wearing the mask. All of this early work should be conducted in silence, with no talking as character or self. As the work progresses, individuals can interact to discover the effect of their developing character on others. Through this, a further understanding of the character emerges. Vocal sounds can be made, but actual words are best avoided, in my experience.

Once masked characters have been developed, scenarios can be planned, but the most illuminating activity comes from placing selected characters in particular situations. These should be fairly archetypal – the park bench; finding a £10 note; the reading of the will; the pea-shooter; the pickpocket. Once again, serendipity brings some of the most exciting results.

It is unlikely that all the masks made by a class will 'work'. The teacher should build up a collection of other masks which can be introduced to supplement them. Particularly effective examples should be added to this collection if they can be prised from their makers!

Chapter 4

THE ROLE OF THE TEACHER
OF DRAMA

Teachers of drama will develop a way of relating to students which allows both parties to feel comfortable whilst preserving the necessary role of 'teacher'. Teachers must gain the confidence and respect of students if drama is to flourish. They must radiate their sense of interest in the material and the subject, coaxing and leading students to discover and appreciate the satisfactions to be gained. Lesson structures must allow the impetus to pass to the students, with the teacher sharing experiences, questioning, challenging assumptions, helping the students evaluate their work and facilitating the frameworks within which it can progress. Dorothy Heathcote describes the teacher of drama as a 'benign manipulator' (in Nixon, 1982, p.40), and it is clear that teacher intervention is almost certain to affect student thinking. Gavin Bolton says that drama should meet 'the pupils' wants and the teacher's intentions' (ibid.), and perhaps this gives a better indication of the balance of responsibility.

Because of the often fine balance between teachers' need to encourage spontaneous, creative and sincere responses from students and the need to establish good working conditions for all, they must be clear in the operation of the following obligations. Many of these will require explicit and concentrated teaching in the early part of the course. All will eventually form part of the underlying code of good practice that should operate in drama lessons, and teachers should not shrink from their application.

Provide structure and order

Educational drama's past is bedevilled by the fallacious notion that nothing should inhibit the free flow of the students' 'self-expression'. It is true that drama does not flourish through teacher domination, but nor will it in a completely non-interventionist atmosphere. The best drama happens within well-defined and mutually understood organization and the teacher should ensure that lessons, especially in the early stages, include instructions that transmit such knowledge. This should include how and when to enter and leave the drama space, changing arrangements, control signals, use of rostra and other technical aids, respect for students' own work and that of others, and expectations of commitment. The drama teacher has few of the securities normally found in the classroom – chairs and tables at which to sit students, exercise books and textbooks to work with – and when things go wrong, drama teaching can feel like the rack. Equally, if the teacher has attended to all the necessary responsibilities outlined below, it can be exhilarating!

Encourage the contemplation of worthwhile material

It is essential that the drama effort is not harnessed to trite content. This is not to say that lessons can contain nothing but 'heavy' issues, simply that the subject matter should be worth the time and effort expended.

Teach the skills, using subject-specific vocabulary

It is only through progressive control of the different facets of the medium that the students' respect and interest for drama's potential and their place within it can develop. The teacher must plan and execute a graduated entry into the world of drama, in all its aspects, explaining and using the technical terms which are special to the medium.

Show a real interest in and respect for students' work

Students can tell whether or not a teacher cares about their efforts. In a subject which often encourages open examination of sensitive issues, it is imperative that the drama teacher display sincere regard for the work in progress. Any teacher not so doing runs the risk of alienating students in ways that will severely limit discussion, practical work and risk-taking.

Extend individuals to the maximum of their abilities

This requires the teacher to create a supportive atmosphere where groups and individuals are challenged to produce work of the highest possible quality. Students should be helped to deepen superficial responses. They will need to take risks at a real operational level – explaining, often tentatively, a complex idea to a group which is capable of scorn, for example – and also within the drama. The teacher should take time to talk to individuals about their work, negotiating approaches to the drama which will take account of the differing interests and abilities of the students.

Engender a caring social attitude

This is essential if the drama is to prosper. Students must accept that all have a right to form and express ideas. The social network of the playground often impinges on this and the teacher must create an atmosphere of trust. Those who seldom contribute or find it difficult to articulate their thoughts must be supported. This requires that insensitive comment from others be positively challenged until all come to accept the humane behaviour pattern that must prevail.

Listen and respond

The teacher will need to take the drama seriously. Students can sense if their teacher has little interest in what they are doing and this can quickly undermine the quality of the activity. Respect should be shown for ideas being garnered from the class. If students feel you are going through the motions of consultation, having already decided what will happen, the exercise is pointless. Teachers need to amplify and clarify some of the ideas which flow from students. They act as a filter if they wish to influence the next stage, identifying and supporting suggestions that have potential for learning. Where students are to make all the decisions, the teacher may simply act as a facilitator for discussion. Where a class has taken to addressing discussion responses to the teacher, she should move away from the speaker, thereby ensuring that all can hear. Encourage individuals to speak to their fellows as well as to you.

Have access to a range of sanctions

The teacher must be prepared to take action when students find it difficult to co-operate with the work in hand. Sometimes the problem is fairly benign, as when someone gets the giggles; at others it is more serious and can cause major damage to the progress of the lesson. Drama lessons require a positive atmosphere, and teachers should avoid becoming too severe in attitude if at all possible. Praise should be given for good work, and the underlying message to miscreants should be: 'We are doing something interesting here and you are hindering that by your behaviour.' Students who cannot co-operate should be sat on one side with the instruction, 'Let me know when you feel able to join in again.' When that signal comes, the teacher should confirm that the problem has passed and that the standard of behaviour required has been understood. Where a more serious breach occurs, the student should be seen at the end of the lesson, and a contract made concerning behaviour in future lessons. At the start of the next session the teacher should discreetly remind the student of the agreement and comment on adherence or otherwise at the end of that lesson. I have found these practices sufficient to deal with almost all problems. Where they do not, there is usually a deep-seated problem which needs a more specific approach from appropriate colleagues in the school.

Ensure that students do not embark on work which seems likely to fail

The teacher must balance the needs of students to try out ideas in action with her own knowledge, born of experience, of what will bring satisfaction and what is safe. A half-hour search for a slide projector and suitable slides for use in a room that has no blackout is a waste of time. Likewise, a structure built of all available rostra and chairs, intended to support the God King, might be downright dangerous as well as unworkable. Intervention to help groups contemplating drama content which is plainly unworkable is more contentious. The teacher must judge whether the group is engaged with interest in the exploration and is 'getting somewhere', or whether it is becoming frustrated and dissatisfied. Ideally, students should be helped to recognize the problem by well-directed teacher questioning:

- Tell me some of the ideas you have discussed.
- Which one do you think you would like to use for your drama?
- Do you think it would help if you got a clearer idea of the story first?
- Why do you think it's not working?
- What do you need to do to get over that problem?

This approach can help the group break the circle of unfruitful exploration without depriving them of the right to make key decisions.

Be flexible in the application of lesson planning

Having prepared lesson material, teachers should critically observe its effect in action, being prepared to dwell longer on a phase that would benefit from more time spent on it, or making decisions about when the work should move on. There should be a willingness to adapt material or structures up to and including the abandonment of the original scheme if circumstances demand it.

Ensure that technical aids are available, safe, and that students know how to use them effectively

The teacher should be a facilitator in this respect. All equipment should be sturdy enough to withstand the wear and tear that constant use will bring. Tape-recorders, blank cassettes, a quiet recording space, rostra, lighting, simple costumes and props, musical instruments and a slide projector and screen should be to hand. Teachers must ensure that equipment use is fairly arranged and that the demands of one group do not unduly interfere with practical work of others.

Be aware of the different strategies for extending work

At the simple level this ranges from knowing how to take apparently completed work and give it life within a new structure (dealt with in Chapter 7), through the sharing of polished drama between classes, straight production work derived from lesson material, to tours and school exchanges, both home and abroad. Day-to-day drama lessons provide the seed-bed from which such ideas grow and students should be encouraged to see the potential for extension within their work.

Be aware of the function of performance

The 'school play' is, rightly, still a regular fixture in the calendar of most schools. Teachers must decide how drama generated by day-to-day curriculum activity can grow into public performance and know how to select, and approach the production of, appropriate published plays.

Represent drama within the school and locality

This is particularly important if drama is to thrive through widespread understanding of its workings. Misconceptions may fill the vacuum left by drama teachers who fail to explain the nature of their subject to colleagues and parents. Appreciation of performance work should exist within a general understanding of the nature of 'non-performance' activity. An annual open evening which explains through demonstration of practice is simple to arrange, and can provide an affirmation of drama for student participants. Publicity for performances should stress how they rest upon a breadth of curriculum work. It is especially important that governors are well informed.

Evaluate the success of organization and teaching strategies

Intelligent reflection on what happens within the lessons and how it can be improved is essential. Awareness of developments in the field and refreshment of their thinking through books, courses, conferences and membership of professional organizations can bring drama teachers into stimulating contact with the wider world of drama. Teachers should keep comprehensive records of their students' progress.

Visit the theatre

Chapter 7 considers the wide variety of models available for performing to others, but it is important that students should also be receivers of other people's drama. Regular theatre visits should be organized, preferably to performances which relate in some way to the drama curriculum. Students' understanding of dramatic language will be extended by witnessing good theatre. Teachers should revitalize their own sense of drama through regular play-going.

Work in role

There are times when the teacher wishes to intervene in the drama as a character within it, managing the educational and dramatic potential of the activity through a related role. This is sometimes expected by the students, as when the teacher plays the factory manager or social reformer in a nineteenth-century industrial scene. At other times the contribution may be unpredictable – the teacher notices that the presence of a newspaper reporter might make the vociferous and domineering official a little more circumspect. There should be clear signals as to when the teacher is in role and when not – a scarf donned, or hat worn, for instance. Teachers should beware of simply indulging through role their own vision of how the drama should progress. Their intervention should be in the best interests of the work in hand, challenging or deepening the students' involvement and not threatening their ownership of the drama.

The simplest way of gaining confidence in role-taking is to adopt the 'help' format. Here the teacher takes the role of an individual with a problem or difficulty, who seeks help from students invested with special knowledge which allows them to give such aid. A suitable role might be that of an old person living alone who has difficulty understanding a letter from a neighbour's solicitor. The letter threatens legal action over a barking dog which is the old person's only companion. Another could be based on a woman who has lost her short-term memory and enlists the students' help in reconstructing who she is from documents, clothing and items contained in a suitcase. Such self-contained roles could be seen as one-off confidence-builders or injected into a story devised by students. Teacher in role can be a useful device for allowing students to organize and communicate newly acquired knowledge – relating aspects of local history to a newcomer in the community; explaining thunder and lightning to an eighteenth-century rustic; helping a soldier seriously injured in the early stages of the First World War to understand what course the war subsequently took.

Rather than role-play very famous people, it can be more helpful to choose a minor character who may have witnessed events from the sidelines – one of the sailors who helped carry Nelson below; the woman who lived next door to the house where Anne Frank was captured. Besides providing an interesting perspective, such roles allow the role-player to plead ignorance of certain questions.

In role, the teacher can make statements or ask questions which will draw explanations in a 'people' context, giving that knowledge human relevance. The role should not be hammed up or students will find difficulty in responding sincerely. A role can be begun by the teacher leaving the room and re-entering in role. Similarly, it can end with an exit. Roles can also be played by other teachers, adults or older students. In general a stronger, more central role is required when working with younger or inexperienced students. Contributions become more subtle and delicate as student proficiency increases.

Not all teachers can or wish to work in role. They see their best contribution as 'nudging', challenging and carefully evaluating the drama from outside it. Do not worry if this is your preferred technique, but if you have never attempted 'teacher in role', do give it a try.

Chapter 5

TECHNIQUES AND APPROACHES

Stages in making drama

These can be broadly characterized as *speculation, exploration, shaping* and *communication*.

When children are asked to explore a particular stimulus, concept or idea, their *speculative* abilities are used in reacting to and unpacking it. If a newspaper article is used as a stimulus, for example, participants will call on their previous experience of the incidents described to ask questions and develop hypotheses. The presentation of the stimulus material must be expertly handled, whether it be story-reading, showing of a photograph or artefact, or the distribution of a case study. Teachers need a sense of drama in the way they describe and present the stimulus. For the drama to be launched successfully, the students' interest and imagination must become effectively engaged with the lesson material at this stage. Much early drama and some in later years may not move beyond this level.

Having created a number of hypotheses in the speculative stage, students create drama models to *explore* situations which will advance or illustrate their thinking. Through discussion and negotiation they modify the chosen models, rerunning them to take account of changing perceptions. Each improvisation is a 'holding form', a representation within the medium of current understandings. The very act of attempting to capture these understandings within the drama changes students' perceptions of them and leads to a further search for effective modelling of their new insight. This 'leap-frogging' is endemic in the drama process and time must be given to allow it to take place.

Having explored the chosen topic, students can use the medium to symbolize more exactly the meaning that has emerged. *Shaping* and crafting the dramatic metaphor to make it a more effective represent-ation of their thinking are aided by an ability to use drama skills. At this stage, the material content does not alter greatly as the students are principally engaged in the aesthetic exercise of using the art form to its best effect.

If they discover material they feel may be of interest to others, they may choose to *communicate* it. This can be as simple as one pair telling another about what transpired, or as complex as a full public performance. More usually it is the sharing of the shaped drama with other class members. This communication is only worth while if the students feel they have something significant to share, a distillation of meaning which has emerged from their close study of the theme. This stage is examined more closely in Chapter 7 , 'Sharing to Performance'.

Content and stimulus

The content of drama lessons may be taken from the full range of human concerns. The only prerequisite is its appropriateness in interesting the class being taught, and its fitness in meeting the aspirations of the teacher and the needs of the students. We do not know why particular topics work with some classes and not with others. The basic requirement is that the material should have potential for drama, and this is the main yardstick teachers appear to apply when selecting content. The teacher of drama should be constantly looking out for, and saving for future use, material of this nature. Drama books are a good source, and some are listed in the Bibliography, but the following stimuli can also be useful:

Photographs

These should require interpretation, rather than be explicit, allowing students to infer story and meaning.

News cuttings

These provide the facts of, say, a crime but not the human detail which is the stuff of drama.

Documents

Letters, wills or postcards, for instance, which require the generation of human detail. Effective-looking old documents can be produced by baking newly made ones in an oven, after first soaking them in tea. Students' imagination can be captured by presenting just fragments of documents.

Objects

These can be an ideal source for story-making. The silver-topped cane – who did it belong to? The small leather purse with the initials – who carried it? These stimuli work best if they are described as being 'not any old cane/purse, but one which has special associations'.

The cane was used by an aristocrat during a memorable incident. The purse was carried by a female survivor of the *Titanic* sinking –

hence its stains. Objects can be used in combination. The Schools' Museum Service can provide artefacts of interest.

Short story or novel extract

Unless the intention is an exact representation of the storyline, be prepared for the drama to move away from its literary beginnings. It is often best to follow the general concepts embedded in the writing:

> *Can you think of another situation in which greed might be the downfall of an ambitious person?*

> *What might happen in a situation like that if the children didn't find the secret door?*

Historical incident

The Peterloo massacre; the Gresford mining accident; depopulation of the Highlands; the Boston Tea Party. The teacher will need to identify what is dramatic about the incident, decide how to serve up the facts effectively and how to organize an exploration of it.

Poem

Most poems condense meaning and, if carefully chosen, lead to a ready focus. Because of their stylized form, many poems work best within non-naturalistic drama forms. A narrative poem may be treated as a story and explored accordingly.

Sound tape

This may have snatches of dialogue, sounds and music. It usually needs to be put in a context that will suggest dramatic tension:

> *This tape was made by the police when they eavesdropped on some criminals.*

> *This tape was found in a watertight container floating near the area in which the boat was last sighted.*

Statistical information

For example, the number of children working in the mines in 1810; the number of children involved in road accidents the previous year; the incidence of 'pet-dumping' after Christmas. Students invent stories which exemplify how the problem affects individuals – the stories behind the statistics.

Interesting compound stimuli can be used such as a number of objects and documents contained in a coat, box or suitcase. The most complex I have used is the creation of a complete room. This takes some time to set up, but can be used over several days, with a number of classes. The 'room' can be created within the drama space, its perimeter being delineated by the use of light, carpet or furniture placement. Once the basic furnishing and lighting have been arranged (which can be fairly skeletal and still work), articles with human association are placed around the room – a wastepaper bin with a screwed-up, partly written letter, a newspaper with a particular story ringed, an address written on the edge of a restaurant menu, a coat over the back of a chair with an auction catalogue in the pocket, a cassette-recorder which is still playing. The items should intrigue but not confuse. It is not necessary for the people devising the room to have a 'story' in their minds – the students will invent this. It is necessary, however, to make sure that the fragments of stimuli placed in the room intrigue the students and are capable of interrelationships – the first name of the victim identified in the ringed newspaper story is the same as the person to whom the screwed-up letter is addressed.

Let each group of four or five spend five minutes in the room for an initial exploration, then ask them to devise what they think happened in the room in the last five or eight minutes before it was vacated. Let them in again later to check their story against the actual environment and to act out their reconstruction. When all reconstructions are completed, share each one with the rest of the class sitting around the edge of the room.

Most stimuli should act as a lift-off rocket to get the students' own ideas into the air. Once this has happened, the stimulus can either be disregarded or integrated into the drama.

Problem drama

I use the term 'problem' to describe the focal energy of the drama. Alternative expressions might be 'dilemma' or 'conflict'. The fact is that drama – and educational drama is no exception – generally looks at the struggle of human beings to live their lives together, with all the pleasures, tensions and moral questions this engenders. Watching two people on stage who never disagree and act out an hour of complete contentment with the world is likely to be very undramatic. Some kind of problem must be introduced if drama is to flow from the situation. Dorothy Heathcote (1971) refers to this principle as 'Man in a mess'. Usually, characters and relationships must be defined before the problem is introduced. The exception to this is where such definition can proceed through the exploration of a dilemma. There are no hard and fast rules, but the teacher of drama must know at what point the problem should be introduced. It is essential that the problem has no easy solution and the teacher must build in factors which inhibit such a course.

Generating feelings

Students should not be told to 'be angry' so that they can experience the feelings of anger. You can only put them in situations where the anger emerges as a result of the life conditions being explored. Failure to observe this simple principle will lead to melodramatic and superficial drama.

Particularization

Students need to particularize the issues being explored if they are to identify with and care about them. In practice this means drama works most effectively when generalizations such as friendship and trust are firmly embedded in the detail of human lives. Superficial work often emerges from 'issue drama' which fails this test.

Groupings

When the instruction 'Get into groups' is given, there is generally a gravitation to friendship bonds. This may be fine for most work, but students should be encouraged to work with a full range of class members, including those of the opposite sex. Lesson beginnings can include exercises which require students to pair with someone with whom they do not normally work, this instruction being repeated each time a new pairing is required. When asking for groups of, say, five, the teacher asks that there should be three boys and two girls or vice versa. This can cause some organizational problems at first, but it is worth persevering until students become flexible in their opinion about who they can or should work with. The teacher will be required to encourage and arbitrate, especially if the class contains social isolates. Care should be taken to handle problems sensitively. Ideally, those who are left over after groups have been formed should be asked, 'Which group would you like to join?' and the social sensitivity of the students should allow such choices to be exercised without protest or fuss. Sometimes the more mature and socially responsible members of a class can be approached outside the lesson to seek their consent to allowing social isolates to work in their, usually successful, groups.

Classes which experience regular drama sessions usually fall into a pattern of predictable groupings. This often stems from considerations of friendship, interest and ability. Where these groupings are to be deliberately disturbed by the teacher, success is aided by the provision of good, supportable reasons:

> *For most of this year you have usually worked in groups made up of the same people. Because I feel you may have forgotten what it is like to work with others in the class, I am going to assign you to new grouping for this next exercise.*

> *This next exercise follows naturally on the one you have just completed and because, in the last one, each group came up with a different solution, it would be useful to have a representative from each of the old groups in each new group.*

> *For the first part of the lesson I want you to work with someone you have not worked with yet this term.*

Cliché

Teachers often worry that their students' drama work is unoriginal. It should be borne in mind that life bombards youngsters with signals of all kinds, especially televisual ones, and it would be surprising if these did not appear in their drama output. Television is an important shared experience, transmitting powerful cultural messages, and teachers should make use of it. What must be avoided is the slavish representation of such material. Rather it should be seen as a springboard from which significant drama can be launched. Students will often deal with archetypal situations through a clichéd response. Unless the genre is being studied in its own right, teachers should lead them beyond this stage, exploring the cliché specifically in some cases, until the students are able to recognize a higher-order response.

Holding form and meaning

When exploring and developing drama through a series of improvisations, discussions and further improvisations, students cannot make leaps from early stages to end-stage without going through the sequence of events which the drama process demands. What was done in week 1 of a three-week project may seem naïve and clichéd when viewed from the more sophisticated stages of later work. This is necessary and unavoidable, and students should be made aware of the development that will occur. The form they are working in at any particular moment is their best way of representing and exploring the issues at that time. It is a holding form, and it will change.

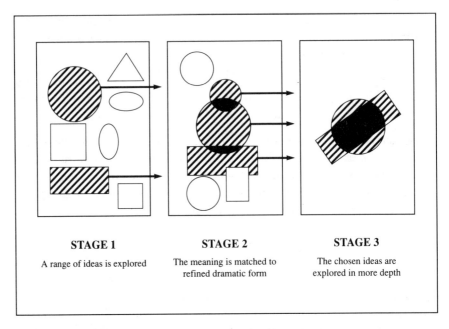

STAGE 1

A range of ideas is explored

STAGE 2

The meaning is matched to
refined dramatic form

STAGE 3

The chosen ideas are
explored in more depth

Figure 5.1 Exploration through dramatic improvisation

Figure 5.1 attempts a representation of the process of exploring ideas through improvisation. In stage 1, a range of ideas may be explored through discussion and practical work. Some of them, represented by the cross-hatched shapes, interest the group and are selected and carried forward for further examination and development in stage 2. The form changes, but so does the meaning which the group thinks it is examining. From this work, further ideas emerge to be carried forward to stage 3. The drama is refined until the meaning the group is shaping most exactly fits the form in which it is being expressed. In this context, students might say, 'Lift your arms more slowly and raise your head with a jerk when you see me' not only because it *looks* better, but because it more exactly represents the meaning the participants are attempting to capture in the drama.

Lesson structure

Getting started

The typical lesson often starts with 'warm-ups'. These almost invariably contain physical and verbal games which are used to stimulate the students and to act as a break between the activity they have just left and the drama they are to be asked to do. Whilst such games have a place, it is important that the teacher knows why they are being used and when they are appropriate. A five-minute tag session where, over the weeks, students are asked to invent a number of release mechanisms may provide the imaginative physical charge for a mime lesson. A word game where students in pairs devise a story through each individual adding single words to the developing narrative can be a valid model for explaining how improvisation works. Used judiciously, such activities have a place. They signal the levels of physical and imaginative energy required in the lessons, allow free use of space and encourage creative response. Used slavishly and unthinkingly they detract from the real business of the lesson. Older students often need to be enlivened by this phase of the lesson, whilst younger ones may require calming down to an acceptable level of concentration.

Perhaps a better way of regarding the lesson's beginning is to see it as a planned preparation for the main focus of the lesson. The teacher may want to practise particular skills to be employed later in the lesson, for instance. In this case, a whole gamut of possible activity suggests itself, including games, discussion, and short drama exercises which include voice and movement warm-ups. Usually this period lasts no more than ten minutes. Whole lessons may be used to teach major skills, but minor ones or recapitulation of major ones can be covered in the first part of lessons. In this way, a graduated skills course can be built for inexperienced students. Sometimes the first part of the lesson is used to give the students experience of the theme which is to be the 'meat' of the lesson. If the class is to look at a poem about friendship, the teacher may have put the students in several improvised situations where this quality or its absence forms the focus of the drama.

Whatever the particular content of the lesson's beginning, it should usually carry the unspoken message: 'We're in drama now, so be ready to work in ways the subject demands'.

If work from a previous lesson is being continued, students may work on it almost from the start of the lesson. Effective contact can be made with the ideas present at the end of the previous lesson by using the 'heads on knees' approach described below.

The focus

The focus of the lesson is intended to energize the drama activity, and should be carefully planned to have maximum effect. Setting up situations which have potential for drama is a skilled business. Students need to be told enough to draw them into the work, but not so much that they need contribute nothing to its development. Stimuli need to be presented to the best effect – slides that can barely be seen due to ineffective blackout or photocopied photographs that are ill defined are of little use.

The focus having been introduced and the students 'hooked', the teacher must provide the circumstances in which the drama can develop. One of the teacher's most important tasks is to monitor the responses of the students, deepening their involvement by appropriate intervention. It is during this period that the original stimulus or idea introduced by the teacher is absorbed by the students who, by their response, make it their own. The teacher needs to allow and encourage this transfer of ownership if the material is to succeed.

Single lessons or series?

Drama lessons can be organized in single units or series. Single, 'one-off' sessions can be useful for covering a range of topics in a short time. Skills can be introduced in this way, or a class can be introduced to the concept of reacting imaginatively to a number of varied stimuli. As the work becomes more sophisticated it is unlikely that it can or should be contained within single lessons. In the primary school, drama activity can be integrated into work in other areas of the curriculum, thus escaping many of the strictures that tend to occur in the secondary phase.

A series of lessons allows more time to explore and develop ideas. Once the students have ownership of challenging drama, many hours can be spent exploring, experimenting, selecting, shaping and sharing. One of the most important judgements the teacher of drama must make is when to move on to the next stage. Flexibility is required to accommodate the differing rates of progress whilst preserving the overall cohesion of the lessons. Certainly the teacher should avoid leaving too little time for students to develop their ideas in action. This applies particularly to work being prepared for sharing. A hastily prepared, shallow drama where things go wrong adds nothing to students' regard for the value of the subject.

Some time should be left at the end of each lesson for participants to reflect on the progress of the work and to make decisions about future directions. This discussion should not be for the purpose of reaching consensus on the ethical and moral issues within the drama – 'So, we all agree, we should be kind to people like this' – but to allow the students a genuine planning role. This can be of great use to the teacher in preparing the next session and in organizing the provision of appropriate resources.

When drama activity is carried over a lesson series, it is essential that students are able to re-establish effective contact with the material and their treatment of it. An effective way of doing this is to sit them down in their own spaces with their eyes closed and heads on knees. Get stillness and silence then talk them through the work of the last lesson, asking them to recall with whom they were working, in which space, which role they played, what happened in the improvisation they last did and what they decided to do this week. You can also inject some 'commitment' advice here:

> *We only have forty minutes left. Remember how we ran out of time last week? We must work really efficiently this lesson if we are to get to the point we agreed to aim for. Remember we said the mime needed to be sharper, and we should avoid moving through the spaces being used by other groups so as not to distract them. The improvisations were some of the best you have done – let's see if we can keep that quality this session.*

Traditionally, lessons began with individual work, then paired, then groups. There is good reason for this, as individuals have to commit themselves to an idea and this can be shared most effectively with one other person before this depth of experience is brought to the group. A more flexible attitude can prevail, however. Making sure each student in a group has an idea can be achieved by giving each two minutes to think of 'the reason the giant did not kill the child' before sharing it in turn with the others. It is necessary to ensure that all feel they have a right to volunteer information. It is possible for particular individuals to dominate the discussion to the extent that others do not bother to contribute.

Stock lesson structures

There are three basic lesson structures which the teacher of drama may find useful. Content can be varied to provide a great number of possible lessons.

Skills lesson

I dealt with the basic skills of drama in Chapter 3. A lesson series can begin with teaching a particular skill – mime, for instance – and once the basics have been mastered, story can be explored. The very exercising of the skill within improvisation generates content for development. Students moving around with masks, feeling the inter-actions between themselves and others will begin to feel story possibilities. Movement work can follow the same pattern. The very act of moving allows the creation of the role, place and subsequent story. The teacher provides the overall structure in which this can happen and the circumstances in which this serendipity can develop. The drama thus develops out of the skill practice.

Lift-off lesson

Students are taken to the point where they have come to understand and feel a set of roles and circumstances. The teacher then introduces a problem which will be the focus of the drama. An example is the development of a youth club, in which the students role play members and adults on the management committee. The roles can be arranged by negotiation, making sure to achieve the correct character balance which the subsequent drama will require. Alternatively, the teacher could hand out role cards for the key roles, allowing the rest of the class to be club members.

When the roles, physical layout, club-night activities and social intercourse of the members have been established through practical work and the students have *identified* with the situation, a problem is introduced. This might be the Council sending a couple of employees to the club to measure the place up. These two know that the Council is considering selling the site for development, but have been told to say nothing. They think they are visiting the club on a non-club night and start to measure up the grounds. The members are allowed to discover their presence quite naturally. The employees do not tell the members why they are measuring up, and when the discussion reaches impasse, the teacher enters in role as a senior planning official.

When the members question her, she is surprised they don't know about the situation, as she maintains a letter was sent to the club some weeks ago. The official says she is not empowered to say anything and goes off to phone her office. On her return she apologizes for the letter not having arrived due to a mix-up in the office. She explains that the Council is due to discuss the future of the club site at its next meeting in three days' time and further apologizes that the club members have not had a chance to make representations. She has previously been primed to offer the members an opportunity to meet the chair of the Planning Committee and the consultant architect.

At this point the teacher stops the improvisation and announces that the meeting will take place in twenty minutes' time. She provides the club members and council employees (who now become the Chair of Planning and an architect), with a map of the area, showing the position of the club in relation to other buildings, especially housing and schools, matters which are particularly pertinent to the club's location. The consultation meeting starts when the teacher, in role as a particularly fussy clerk, invites the members into an ante-room to the Council chamber. She explains that a young wives' organization normally plays badminton in the space and that the youth club people are very lucky to have the use of it, and particularly lucky to be given some of the time of the very important Chair and architect. The officials arrive and explain what the Council is contemplating. They feel the youth club site is valuable prime development land and the Council has an obligation to make money from its assets. The Council is considering building a much-needed leisure centre on the site, to be run by a private company. The club members will be asked to merge their club with another two miles away.

There follows a period of questions to the officials – perhaps twenty minutes – before the clerk, reminding the members how privileged they have been to have a hearing, tells the officials they are needed in the chamber for the discussion about the land. This is the point of lift-off, and the drama can now go different ways. The officials might return to announce the Council's decision, which, depending on the outcome, could lead the story forward – a decision to build, exciting further action by members; consulting lawyers; talking to the other club about overcrowding; organizing a petition; visiting their ward councillor – or a decision not to build; action to secure the club's future should it be so threatened again – or a deferred decision pending the club's right to present its case properly; organization of the case and its presentation. The students might also wish to improvise the council meeting where the outcome is decided.

I have seen this format adapted for a cross-curricular project in a middle school where a class created a coastal town in an area of outstanding natural beauty. The students developed material on the ecology, economics, geography and history of the area, family structure and employment pattern. They built relief models, created a newspaper and generally acted out the lives of the inhabitants. Once they had identified with the place and its way of life, the teacher introduced an official-looking letter which informed the inhabitants that the government was considering building a submarine base close to the town. This would mean a doubling of the population and the destruction of a large area of beautiful landscape. On the plus side were the defence needs of the country and the fillip the development would give to the town and its business.

Students worked on the potential effects on their town for two weeks. The work culminated in the arrival of an 'Inspector' to conduct a public inquiry. When he arrived, he was met outside the school by delegations wishing to present their points of view. Placards were waved, and protest messages hung in the top-floor windows of the building.

The lift-off occurs after the students have identified with a set of circumstances and the characters within them. Once the problem is introduced, the drama should have a life of its own, with the teacher simply making best use of what comes, supporting, and sometimes steering a little, the material which flows. Occasionally the teacher needs to intervene to create fresh impetus for the drama and she must be aware of the points at which such intervention will have most effect.

Backtracking lesson

This approach requires the students to reconstruct the lives of people through an examination of available evidence. The evidence is usually in the form of documents and objects which carry strong human association and some suggestion of a problem to be explored. An example of material of this kind, suitable for Year 9 and above, is shown below.

Dear Chris,

It was good to see you on Thursday after so long. It was a shame you didn't meet Phil – perhaps next time.

I feel we got somewhere in the end but I can't help feeling you left thinking our problems are far from being solved.

Please don't rock the boat now – bears care remember?

Jen

P.S. You left this letter behind – do we have to stoop to issuing frighteners to each other?

Davis Priest Parkin & Co.

Tollgate House,
CROWBOROUGH, SUSSEX.

SOLICITORS

D.R. Davis T.D., D.L.
J.R. Nott.   M.R. Priest T.D.
M. Markham   K Larner
NOTARIES PUBLIC   L. Kitson   P.M. Carter-Flock
COMMISSIONERS FOR OATHS

Telephone : Crowborough 5216

And at Lewes (Tel. 3721)
And at 3, Old Square, Lincolns Inn, WC2

MM/PW

23 November, 1993

Ms J Stevens
12 Longville Gardens
Aylesbury
Bucks

Dear Ms Stevens,

I am writing to advise you that I still await a reply to my letter of August
29th. I would also remind you that, as per our agreement at our recent
meeting in this office, if matters are not satisfactorily resolved by the end
of this month, the normal processes of the law must take their course.

Yours sincerely,

Martin Markham

M MARKHAM

Students, working in pairs or threes, read the two letters. Through discussion, they 'backtrack' on the events that led up to the situation suggested in the letters, and simultaneously develop a sense of the individuals involved. When they have placed the people and documents in a satisfactory 'life setting', the teacher asks them to think of an improvisation which would, when acted out, help them to discover more about the people, their relationships and the dilemmas they confront. This can be extended to two or three more improvisations, until the group has a rounded grasp of the individuals, the problems suggested in the documents and the incidents that led to the writing of them. Given time to reflect on what they have reconstructed, the groups may wish to communicate a statement about their findings to the rest of the class through the use of narration, acting out, characters speaking direct to the class or other suitable techniques. This approach can be adapted to render a large variety of lessons suitable for any age. The essential strategy is to provide a set of circumstances which suggest people, place and problem. This must be skeletal and leave scope for interpretation. The skill once more is to provide enough to intrigue, but not so much as to make the material prescriptive.

65

Two other examples may serve to clarify the approach. A cigar box or other appropriate between-the-wars container is filled with the following late Victorian objects: a dried flower head; a feather; a brooch; a birthday card carrying a picture of a beautiful woman with a verse:

> May happiness your soul inspire,
> and bring to you your heart's desire.

and the following inscription:

> Just to wish you many happy returns of the day
> Read carefully the verse on the other side,
> and accept a small token of friendship from me,
>   yours sincerely,
>   Florence.

There is also a photograph of a garden party and a portrait photograph taken just after the turn of the century. It shows a mustachioed male, aged around 25. A letter, handwritten in script of the time, reads:

> Dear Florence
>   Great news! You know I told you that I had written to my Uncle Richard in Vermont—well I heard from him this morning, and he tells me that if I come prepared to work hard, there may be an opening for me. Florence this could be the chance I have been looking for. I know that after what I have been through I could never stay in Bleadon, but one day, when I've made my fortune, perhaps I will return.
>
>   I have managed to get a berth on the liner 'Oriole' which sails this Friday and as there are some affairs to be attended to in London I leave for there this afternoon. Mother is informing anybody that my birthday celebrations are cancelled. I regret that this robs us of an opportunity to meet again, but I know that after our discussion at the garden party on Saturday you will be pleased for me.
>
>   Thankyou for helping me to see things so clearly I will write to you from America when I am settled in.
>
>   Yours affectionate friend
>   Peter

The container is tied with a ribbon. Under the ribbon is a piece of newspaper, roughly torn from a local paper. It carries the item shown below:

Bleadon woman found dead

A 90-year-old woman was found dead at her home, in Castle Street, on Saturday night. Miss Florence Seager was found lying in the house by the police and firemen, who had been called to a living room blaze. It is believed that Miss Seager may have suffered a heart attack and died.

To allow several groups to work on the material, the box should be duplicated, keeping the contents broadly the same. Students are told that this box was found in a chest of drawers at an auction saleroom. They are asked to reconstruct aspects of the lives of the people suggested by the material. As in the example given earlier, they are then invited to create improvisations which would aid their exploration of the developing story.

I have used this material in my teaching. Students devise different contexts in which the artefacts are embedded, but a description of the elements in one which was created recently may show how dramatic story flows from the box's use. This story concerns a woman, Florence Seager, who met Peter in Bleadon when they were young. They met again at the garden party and, after Florence had helped him to come to terms with his father's rejection, which included sacking him from the family firm, Peter invited her to his birthday party. She is greatly attracted to him, and she feels he is to her, though nothing explicit was said, so it is a great shock when he writes to say the party is off because he is going to America. She did not see him again before he left. Ever since, she has kept items to do with him and the garden party. She never married, and the inference is that she never sent the birthday card.

A basic scenario like this can become more detailed as a result of the improvisations used to explore it. The work can be extended in a number of ways, including taking it to full performance.

Teachers of drama should experiment with inventing such packages. They can be tried out in one class, then refined for further use. Jumble sales, junk shops and auctions are ideal places for picking up objects.

67

Care should be taken in making the documents look authentic, although students can be forgiving of photocopied originals.

It is essential that students do not look for one solution to the 'mystery', and they should be encouraged to give full rein to their imaginations. Such drama can be accompanied or followed by research into the period, including social mores. Creative writing could produce further correspondence and documents. Once the principles involved in creating such compound stimuli are understood, students will enjoy devising some themselves.

Role cards

These allow the transmission of detailed information about the character to be played and the context in which that character will operate. They can be useful where the teacher wishes to introduce a range of different roles and wants to save briefing time. They are also employed when the teacher does not wish individuals to know the details of roles other than their own. The following secondary-level cards describe a situation where a teenager's conflicting loyalties to parent and friends are explored:

Elizabeth Price – age 40 – mother

You are a single parent with a 15-year-old son, David.

You have tried to face up to David's approaching age of majority, giving him more freedom in his social life. You do, however, have strict views on under-age drinking – your marriage was ruined by your ex-husband's alcohol addiction. You have introduced David to sherry, wine and shandy at home on the understanding he will not go into pubs without you.

At work you have heard from the father of one of David's friends that this man's son was breathalysed on Sunday night by the police and has been charged with drunken driving. The colleague also tells you that David was in the car and they were 'all a bit merry'.

As part of an agreement, David has his own front-door key and let himself in last night after you were in bed and asleep. You did not hear him come in.

As you return from work on Monday you are told by a neighbour that David was brought home in a police car in the early hours of Monday morning.

The scene starts at 7.30 p.m. on Monday when you call David from his bedroom into the kitchen to discuss matters.

David Price – age 15 – son

You are an only child, living with your mother, Elizabeth. Your father left home two years ago after rows about his drinking habits. You get on pretty well with your mother but you are finding the agreement you have with her about not drinking alcohol outside the house difficult to stick to as your friendship group includes several 17- and 18-year-olds who visit pubs regularly.

On Sunday evening your whole group agreed to meet in a pub before going on to a party. You went too and chipped in to buy a bottle of whisky – everyone else did. You didn't drink any whisky at the party, but you did drink two small cans of beer – there were no soft drinks available. Most people at the party were over 18.

You travelled to the party with Ian, a 17-year-old friend. He seemed to drink a lot, but as the party was twelve miles from your home you had little alternative to getting a lift back with him. On the way home the car was stopped and Ian was breathalysed. The reading was positive and Ian and his passengers were taken to a police station. You gave a statement and after some delay you were given a lift home in a police car. You have your own front-door key so you let yourself in and did not see your mother. You were scared to mention anything about the incident in the few minutes you spent with your mother at Monday breakfast time before you went to school and she to work.

The scene starts when your mother calls you from your bedroom into the kitchen when she returns from work at 7.30 on Monday.

The cards presume basic improvisation skill. The improvisation can be run to its end-point or stopped near the end and the characters questioned in role. The work can be extended by back-tracking on some scenes – the scene in the police station when David admits to drinking and divulges his age, or projecting the story into the future – David meets his Dad on a regular weekend visit and tells him about the incident, for instance. The gender of each role can be changed to suit.

The cards on pages 70 and 71 are suitable for juniors. They can be used to introduce a school situation which focuses on similar issues but in a context relevant to the age-group.

Laura Collier – age 10

You have been best friends with Emily Davis since you both started school. You have been to each other's birthday parties, shared family holidays and often slept at each other's houses. Polly, a new girl in your class, asked Emily round to her house to play last Sunday – you weren't invited. They ignored you for a whole lunch hour yesterday and in class Polly told you some information about your Dad being in danger of losing his job – something you had only told Emily after she had sworn an oath of secrecy.

After school yesterday you asked Emily if she would like to come ice-skating on Saturday but she said she is having Polly round to tea and then they are watching videos together. She invited you, but you were a bit put out and you stormed off in a huff.

You sat next to Emily as usual during morning school but you didn't talk to her. Polly kept looking across at you both and smiling. You poked your tongue out at her.

At morning break you decide to have it out with Emily.

The scene starts when you walk up to her as she sits on a bench in the playground.

Students should be asked to absorb the information contained on their cards before placing them to one side. The cards should not be held or placed as 'prompts' during the subsequent improvisations, although they may be returned to for reference. The content of the card should provide the information required by participants before an improvisation starts. This is dealt with in detail under 'Improvisation' in Chapter 3.

Talk-through

In the early stages of drama, particularly with young children, the teacher can take the students into drama by narration. The story is told slowly and with appropriate pauses to allow the students to act out the implied action. As the work progresses and the students become more confident, the teacher leaves more and more of the decision-making to them. Such a story might begin:

> *Jiffy the dog was curled up on the floor fast asleep. As the letterbox clattered, the dog stretched out all its legs and its neck, and reared*

Emily Davis – age 10

You have been friends with Laura Collier since you started school together. You have been to each other's birthday parties, shared family holidays and often slept at each other's houses. Polly, a new girl in your class, has been trying to be friends with you for some days now. Your parents are friends with hers and your Mum has told you to be nice to Polly as she is unhappy at leaving her old school and all her friends there. You were invited to Polly's house last Sunday and your Mum said you must invite her back this Saturday. You agree reluctantly even though you wanted to go ice-skating with Laura. You invite Laura to tea as well, and to watch some videos, but she storms off in a huff.

Polly's Dad works at the same place as Laura's father and Polly told you Laura's Dad might lose his job as the firm is making people redundant. Laura had already told you that, but you didn't let on to Polly as you had sworn an oath of secrecy to Laura never to tell anyone.

Today Laura has not spoken to you even though she sits next to you in class. Before school you told Polly that Laura was your best friend and that she would have to be friends with her as well. During morning school Polly smiled at Laura a few times, trying to be friendly, but you saw Laura stick her tongue out at her.

At morning break you are a bit fed up with them both and you sit on a bench in the playground to decide what to do.

The scene starts as Laura comes up to talk to you.

---

up on its hind legs to see who was at the door. It was the postman, so Jiffy trotted out to smell the letters. There had once been a special offer in a little parcel from a dog-food firm, and Jiffy always checked to see if another one came.

This is very highly structured and does not require the students to make major decisions within the drama. Later, sequences such as:

But then the dog saw something that made its hackles rise, and it quickly hid behind a tree-stump to decide what to do next. Having thought of a plan, Jiffy started to put it into action.

Here, the overall story structure is governed by the narration, but the decision on what individuals see and what they will do about it is left to them. This technique can be adapted for other use – in pairs, A narrates whilst B acts out, then change over roles.

71

Freeze-frame

Sometimes called a 'depiction', it occurs when students hold a particular moment in the drama. This can be replaced by a 'still photograph' where two-dimensional representation is required.

Tableaux

Similar to freeze-frames, but with the potential for adaptation. One such is to ask students to form a tableau on a particular theme by the gradual addition of individuals to it. This could be a statue – a war memorial for example; or a split-second from life – 'the fairground thief'. After agreeing the general 'feel' of the tableau, the students sit around the construction area in a large circle. After gaining silence, stillness and concentration, the class create the tableau by joining it one at a time. This ensures that no individual joins it without contemplating what the previous person has added to the meaning. Notwithstanding this, with a large group, the building must be fairly brisk to avoid the idea dragging or those already in the tableau being unable to retain their position. To avoid the latter and to keep the shapes well defined, the teacher can offer those in the tableau a chance to relax from their chosen positions, shake out their muscles and return to position. When the tableau is completed, the students should be asked to sharpen its shape in detail, including facial expressions, before it is dissolved. The idea can be extended in a number of ways. One such is to ask the students to bring the tableau alive through improvisation. To define their tableau roles more clearly for others, each can be asked to take up position in role and explain to the rest of the class who they are and what they are doing at the precise moment depicted. This allows others in the tableau to decide who they might interact with when it is brought alive.

Once a tableau has been created, it can be treated as a statue or representation which emerges from a block of stone or some other material. To achieve this the students take up positions close to one another, making a depersonalized mass to represent the modelling material. To the sound of music, the statue gradually unfolds to completion. The music – percussion in the early stages is best – acts as a control to co-ordinate the movement. While the moves are being developed, the teacher can count slowly to an agreed number to allow the group to work out the timing of the statue's creation. For greater effect, or to integrate such techniques into performance, the uncut modelling material can be made more neutral by using only weak light on it, raising the level to full by the time the statue is complete. Coloured material, which becomes visible as the statue grows, can be attached to the front of figures. A class of students can be split into groups to develop tableaux on different aspects of the same theme. On a First World War theme, six groups might accomplish the following.

Group 1: a tableau depicting the international tension which led to war;
Group 2: a depiction of recruitment and soldiers leaving home;
Group 3: an idealized picture of what warfare would be like – a war memorial, for example;
Group 4: the reality of trench warfare;
Group 5: the soldiers' return – victory parade;
Group 6: the reality for some whose menfolk have not returned.

These statues could be linked and accompanied by music made by the students – humming 'Goodbye Dolly, I must leave you' for Group 2's work, singing the chorus of 'Land of Hope and Glory' for Group 3, for instance. Words could be worked in too – 'See you soon, Dad', etc. in Group 2; simple statistical information on casualties in Group 4 – or a complete narration which uses the tableaux for illustration. All such accompaniment is best delivered by students not involved in the tableau under formation.

This is a good example of how quite simple drama exercises can be extended into relatively sophisticated statements.

Forum theatre

An acted-out scene or incident, during which participants or observers are allowed to stop the action in order to change its direction, take over roles, question characters about their motives, or influence the drama in other legitimate ways. A kind of drama laboratory.

Hot-seating

A technique where one or more people are set in character in front of the rest of the class, which questions them. Questioners can deliver their questions in role. A technique for deepening the characters' sense of self, elucidating parts of the jigsaw of facts generated by improvisation and adding complexity to story and motivations.

In a drama concerning a burglary, for instance, students – as themselves – might question the victim, the burglar and the probation officer who has been responsible for the burglar since his/her last court appearance. In work that involves exploration of a local council's decision to sell parkland to a developer for the provision of a shopping complex, students – as regular users of the park – could question the developer, council leader and a protest campaign leader.

Thought-tracking

The speaking of inner thoughts by characters at an agreed signal:

> *When I touch you on the shoulder, I want you to tell us why you did it.*

> *When Sally gives you the truth stuff you are going to tell us your real reason for being in the caves.*

> *As the light falls on you in the tableau, speak your thoughts about the Queen's decree.*

This technique is useful in discussing subtext or in deepening students' understanding of the feelings of characters involved in the drama. It can be linked to others – listening to the thoughts of figures in a tableau; questioning characters who are frozen at the start or end of an improvisation, for example.

Silent movies

Because they bridge the gap between mime and spoken drama, silent movies can provide an effective approach to physical expression. It helps if the teacher possesses a silent film on video to be used as a stimulus for this work.

Suitable recorded music is required to accompany the films created, e.g. *Piano Party* by Winifred Atwell. The flicker effect can be achieved by the use of a home-made wheel attached to the front of a lantern. A disc of hardboard with four holes in it is fixed so it will rotate on a further piece of hardboard with a similarly sized hole. This is shaped to slide into the gel runner on the lantern. Such a device can be rotated by hand or driven by a small electric motor. This arrangement is much more satisfactory than a strobe light, but the latter can be used in the absence of a wheel. Do not use a strobe in classes where any student suffers from epilepsy.

Begin by asking individual students to explore scenarios through improvisation. These should be archetypal – the 'little' victim who ends up on an ice rink by mistake; the same character in a zoo where every animal seems able to escape; the 'sticky cake delivery person' on a hot day. Students should be able to sense the control the music can have on the drama, particularly in the scene's climax and the build-up to it. More complex scenes can be explored in pairs or threes – delivering the piano to the grand house with just too narrow a front door; delivering the new sheet of glass for the shopfront; customer and hairdresser, where the hairdresser's chair has leather straps to restrain ankles and wrists, and the tools are a little unusual; the customer who thinks he is at the chiropodist's, when he is actually in the dentist's surgery. The teacher will need to discuss the implications of not having recourse to speech. The work will need exaggerated facial expressions and physical movements.

More complex scenarios can be devised, and captions can be made to be displayed at appropriate moments. If you are lucky enough to be able to find a good pianist, scenarios can break free of the recorded accompaniment through the use of custom-made music.

Shadow work

This relates well to silent movie approaches. A large screen is required with some back lighting. Scenarios are best kept simple. Coloured gels in back lights can give dramatic effects, and all scenery and props and some costume – hats for example – can be two-dimensional. Much of this can be cut from cardboard boxes. Stories can be narrated whilst being acted out in shadow form. Try experimenting with different light sources. An overhead projector will provide not only light but scenic form and text on the screen. Juxtaposition of students in relation to screen and light source brings characters of different sizes, allowing the creation of giants and huge omnipotent hands. Try integrating shadow scenes, as dreams or nightmares, into naturalistic drama.

Puppetry

Puppetry is the Cinderella of drama, a throwback to the craft lessons of the post-war primary school. I believe it can make a significant and valuable contribution to drama in both primary and secondary phases.

Rod and glove puppets are the easiest to make and use as students can learn to make and manipulate them very quickly. Marionettes are usually not suitable for whole-class lessons.

Puppets can be made from a surprisingly wide range of materials. Inanimate objects such as oranges, sunglasses and hats can be used in their own right, whilst upside-down plastic drinks or detergent bottles can be given clothes and faces quite readily, even by very young children. These can be manipulated more easily if a stick is Sellotaped into the open neck. Differently shaped bottles or fruit tend to suggest discernible character types and this can be reinforced by suitable attachments – the orange with punk hair and sunglasses; the banana with blonde hair and ruby lips. One of the most effective puppet stories I have ever seen was played out by four differing paintbrushes, each with a suitable paper face stuck on the metal band just below the bristles, which then became hair. Finger puppets are fun, although difficult to see at a distance.

Glove puppets are simple to make. Body size should be adjusted to suit the hand size of different age-groups and a template may help younger students get the right shape. Stitch or glue the two halves of the puppet to each other with the right sides together, then turn inside-out. Details such as hair and face should be glued in place and the head stuffed to give it form, leaving a socket for the index finger. Sock puppets are easily manipulated by young students. A snake-like puppet can be made very quickly by gluing eyes and mouth to a sock. More sophisticated figures enable the whole of the arm below the elbow to be covered, giving an upright puppet which can have a skirt added, or wings for a bird.

Perhaps the most successful puppet form for students of all ages is the rod puppet. A suitable frame for this is shown in Figure 5.2a.

Joints can be made with wire (as shown in Figure 5.2b) or with string. The head is made of folded stiff card glued to the central dowel rod. With young students, the teacher may need to provide a kit with all materials cut to size and holes drilled. Scraps of material of all textures and colours can be used for dressing the frames. Clothing can be stapled, pinned and glued to the body. The face is best drawn on a separate piece of paper, as this allows experimentation before the final choice is glued in place. A dressed puppet is shown in Figure 5.2d. Card hands can be glued to the arms. The frames can be undressed for further use at the end of a project.

A booth can be constructed by the use of two lighting stands with a cross-piece between them. The cross-piece is best made from a scaffold pole with a spigot which will fit a stand fixed to each end. A curtain or blanket can be draped over this, and the height adjusted to suit the students. If you have the stands, and another cross-piece and curtain, a higher, blank surface can be created as a backing to the puppets, but in the absence of this, perform against a plain wall.

A narrator can carry the story, the puppeteers may create their own voices or, most effectively, the two techniques can be used in combination. Live or recorded musical accompaniment, the use of cut-

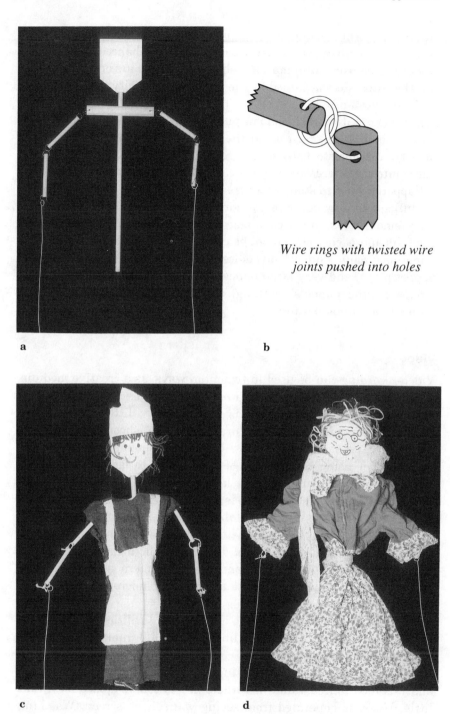

*Wire rings with twisted wire
joints pushed into holes*

a

b

c

d

Figure 5.2 Rod puppets

out scenery which can be held in place by a puppeteer, hooked to the front of the booth or pinned to the backdrop, can enhance the work. The use of simple front illumination helps pick out colours on the puppets, but the chief effect is gained by the puppets' simplicity, and the power of the storytelling.

Experimentation with shadow puppets with articulated limbs, used directly behind a screen or on the platter of an overhead projector, may be appropriate with small groups. Pieces of lighting gel introduced into the figures and scenery can be effective.

Puppetry enables students to create fantastic storylines that might be difficult to play out through normal drama techniques – boys can play female roles, and vice versa; the magic horse can discover the thief. Its approaches should not be confined to the primary school. The sometimes zany humour of adolescents can find a ready home in puppet plays, and very large puppets, their student holders partially hidden by the puppets' clothing, can break free of the booth and interact with human actors.

Video

Video-recording can be used in two main ways: as a creative medium in its own right, and to produce a record of drama work in process for replay and evaluation. There is usually very little time or the equipment to edit videotaped drama, so the shooting should be planned to take account of this. Sequences should be recorded in correct order using the controls of the camera to fade in and out of scenes. Once a fade-out on a scene has taken place, the recorder can be switched off whilst the next scene is prepared. Music and narration can be dubbed on later, but an acceptable soundtrack accompaniment can be achieved by playing a cassette-recorder near the microphone. Getting good-quality recording of dialogue is the biggest problem. In close-ups, the built-in microphone on the camera should be good enough, but for longer-range work an extension microphone should be positioned close to the action.

Modern recorders have a range of high-tech facilities which should ensure effective recording and titling. As with all drama, however, the maxim is: keep it simple.

Except as a means of evaluating performance work, videoing for analysis has limited value. Recorders are so commonplace now, that little *frisson* is generated from seeing yourself on screen. Watching recorded practical work eats into precious practical time, so the teacher should be sure the purpose is worth while.

Photography

The transitory nature of drama is one of its key characteristics. Too often, we miss the opportunity to capture effective images which could be helpful in providing general stimulus to the students and good publicity for drama in the school and community. With the use of colour photocopiers, large images can be produced quite cheaply. Black-and-white prints are equally effective and cost less. Encouraging students to make and process their own films cuts the cost. Cameras which provide instant prints can be effective if the photographs are integrated into the drama as mug shots, family groupings or newspaper photographs, for example.

Drama often makes use of projected images, and it is useful to have a large area on which these can be created. One wall of the drama space painted white, or a white curtain which can be drawn across when required, will suffice. Images can be projected on to surfaces such as rostra sides, suspended screens, commercial tripod screens or even human beings if they are dressed in light clothing. A simple copying table, camera and a fast slide film will allow students to make slides of photographs. Gobos, the cut-out plates which fit lantern gates, will produce less literal imagery on walls, screens and floors. A stage cloth or sheets of light-painted hardboard taped together provide surfaces that vary the predictable colour of the drama-space floor.

Ritual and ceremony

Drama, ritual and ceremony are inextricably linked. Moments of collective importance to a culture are marked with ceremony which almost always displays a strong sense of drama – state funerals; the opening of the Olympic Games; the Nuremberg rallies; coronations. Rituals are carried out with exact repetition to achieve the outcomes the culture associates with the rites – an American Indian rain dance; English harvesters crying the neck; Incas tethering the sun. Students can explore the meaning of ritual in ancient and contemporary cultures through practical work. Teachers might raise the topic through the enactment of a documented ancient ritual and further explore it in modern-day equivalents. Ritualistic and ceremonial elements to do with dress, special objects, music, vocabulary and patterns of speech should be identified and deployed in devising new forms.

Chapter 6

WORKING WITH DRAMATIC TEXT

Play texts have a chequered place in the history of educational drama. For many years doing drama implied reading plays around the class and it is still possible to discover, in the dark recesses of some school stock cupboards, sets of plays quite inappropriate for use in the late twentieth century.

With the widespread adoption of educational drama practice, the scripted play failed to find a regular place in the drama curriculum. This was partly due to the lack of suitable texts, but chiefly to the drama movement's belief that it should resist the dominance of the prepared script and encourage the kind of pupil-generated work it saw as central to successful drama teaching. Most teachers of drama now have a more rounded view, based on a clearer understanding of the relevance of performance.

The nature of script and text

Play scripts are proposals for drama, not the drama itself. Whilst we cannot expect to perform, or see in performance, every play we might work on, we should remember that the script is shorthand for action, and when playwrights create it, they intend the words only as an incomplete record of the pictures, voices, glances and other images that were in their minds when the play was being written. In this respect scripts are like musical scores. The notation represents the sounds the composer hears, but are not the sounds themselves. Music only lives when musicians transform the marks on the page into sound. The notation of scripts, likewise, requires realization in action to become dramatic texts.

'Increasingly, the word "text" is being extended beyond the written page to describe a wide variety of readable sign systems' (Hornbrook, 1991, p.48). These, often culturally specific, signs must be capable of being read by audiences within that culture. They include voice, gesture, movement, music, timing, humour, tension and knowledge of archetype. It is allowable therefore to speak of reading both the script and the text. The processes of a playwright imagining text and creating script, and its recreation in space and time as text, can be represented in Figure 6.1.

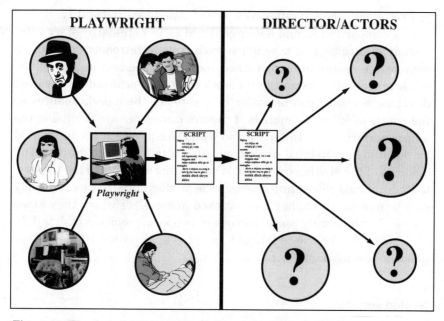

Figure 6.1 The playwright's imagery must be reinvented by the director

The playwright imagines all the richness of the action in her mind – a text; but, unless the performers are able to have the playwright present at rehearsals, she passes on only the words spoken, a notation in written form – a script. With the help of stage directions, it is the director's and actors' job to create the dramatic text, a context with characters who might believably speak these words. The audience engages in another act of interpretation, translating the complex symbols of the dramatic form. When we watch a play, 'we translate the complex semiology of what we see and hear into something meaningful' (Hornbrook, 1991, p.109).

Introducing texts

Once students are confident enough of their own dramatic skills and abilities to perceive themselves as drama practitioners, they should be introduced to the drama of others. This process usually starts with an appreciation of the work of other members of the class, progressing to exposure to that of students in other classes and schools, although it will also probably involve the work of adult actors. This should be achieved in the spirit of comparing the students' use of the medium with the use others have made of it, and all should see themselves as practitioners, albeit at differing levels of experience and ability.

This comparison should not be confined to, or necessarily start with, a study of scripts. It can be more productive to introduce students to appropriate drama in performance, looking at the text as part of the whole process of appreciating the work of writers, actors, designers and directors. Students can be better helped to see these performances as the efforts of fellow dramatists if theatre companies are invited to the school, performing in the space and with the equipment normally used by the students. Related workshops give insight into the practice and opinions of the visiting company. When taking students to the theatre, teachers should choose and research the production with care. The play may be one on which they have worked in detail, or where they know the plot but have only worked on one or two vital moments in detail. In all cases, the approach should be: 'Let's see what these fellow practitioners make of this play.'

Writing scripts

We should not underestimate the skill required to write in the speech genre. Scripts written by youngsters are often stilted and short, and they can be glaringly unsatisfactory in performance. It may be possible to introduce the topic in such a way that these pitfalls are avoided, but it is my belief that the process of generating dramatic text works best when it is closely linked to the use of dramatic action. National Curriculum English requires students to know, at Levels 6 and 9 of the writing attainment target, the differences between spoken and written language, and script-writing is an ideal way of dealing with this topic (NCC, 1989a, pp.14, 6e, 9d).

One way of developing understanding of the nature of spoken language is to develop script from improvisation. Students create and polish an improvised scene before tape-recording it. A transcript of this recording serves as a working document, with subsequent amendments and rewrites tried out in action. The finished script should be typed up and contained in a simple binding, for in this form it stands better comparison with scripts that have been professionally produced. As students become more skilled they may benefit from writing first before trying out their ideas in action. This approach is appropriate when the play is the work of an individual and not a group. In the early stages short pieces of script should be enacted, the writer noting reactions from actors and others before attempting redrafting and the development of further material. To avoid writing a complete play, or as a stage on the way to doing so, detailed scenes of particular interest and potential can be written within a skeletal, whole-plot scenario.

Such scripts can be enacted by students other than those who originated them. A productive way of doing this is to compare a new rendition of the script with the enactment of the authorial group. This raises the concept of interpretation, a matter which can be considered with the playwrights to hand, something usually denied us. Use and development of these techniques can lead to a positive, critical consideration of text in performance, and an awareness of such issues as the roles of the actor and director, and interpretive licence.

Students used to these approaches should be introduced to appropriate texts from other sources. Being playwrights, actors and directors themselves, they are more likely to understand the function and purpose of script generated elsewhere, and to avoid elevating the status of these works to the detriment of themselves.

Subtext

Scripts carry an overt surface meaning which can usually be discerned from a thorough reading. There are often other meanings below the literal, and these are known as the subtext. A line such as 'My! You're looking good today' might mean just that and be delivered as a genuine compliment. If it carried subtext it could have a number of meanings, including: 'I fancy you; You look a mess; You don't usually; Are those your mother's furs?' Students should gain an understanding of subtext through the enactment and creation of simple illustrations before progressing to more complex examples. National Curriculum English requires the study of subtext (NCC, 1989a, p.33).

Directing

The director should have a vision of how the script can be realized in action. Students should be encouraged to make decisions on how they would stage a play and to put some of those decisions into practice, especially by the direction of very short extracts. Educational drama makes regular use of directorial skills when students shape improvised work for sharing. Within what is usually a group process, it is less common for a student to have major control of directing a piece. It is essential that this opportunity is provided and one way of achieving it is to allow students to direct material they have written before progressing to direct the work of their fellows. Teachers of drama must judge when their students are ready for the challenge of directing. Too early exposure to it can result in frustration for all involved. But it is not just a skill to be acquired in late secondary schooling; I have seen very skilled directors in primary schools.

Interpretation

All scripts are capable of reinterpretation. The most profound ones are reworked time and again as directors find contemporary relevance in them. Sophocles' and Shakespeare's plays examine crucial aspects of the human condition, and they endure because they deal with issues which have intrigued humans since the dawn of time, and to which there are no easy answers. Plays of real quality escape the detail of their cultural context to live again in our time.

When working on published text it is essential that the material is seen only as a working document. If copyright is not infringed, photocopies should be used, which the students can annotate as they gain ownership of the material.

The teacher should encourage students to have a valid personal interpretation of the text in action. They should be reminded that, although it is possible to misread a text – to miss the meaning the playwright has buried in it – there is no one definitive form to its reinterpretation for performance. This can be illustrated by showing scenes from two differing videoed productions of the same play – the Michael Hordern and Laurence Olivier *King Lear*s, for instance.

Text can be represented as an iceberg. The written words are the tip of the berg, visible above the water. They rest upon a very large base of feelings and motivations, attitudes and relationships, which must be explored if the enacted words are to become more than an animated reading. The words are only the visible representation of all those aspects of human behaviour, and unless they spring convincingly from an understanding of the submerged base, they will rarely convince.

The following exercises may help teachers to get started in bringing text alive. They can be adapted to suit age-group, text and intention.

1   Students should generally read the text over a short period to judge its shape and effect. There is often no better way of blunting students' interest than by taking ten weeks to read and analyse a text in lessons. Students should be encouraged either to make brief notes on their first reading reactions, and/or to reread the text while jotting down more reflective thoughts. These notes need not be of the 'I understand and know' kind. They can be very tentative and record things which the reader does not 'know', but finds intriguing, contradictory or confusing. They may be framed in the

form of questions. Students should be encouraged to feel for meaning, reading parts of the text aloud to try out different interpretations. These early reactions should be shared and discussed in groups. The notes can be used as *aides-mémoire*.

2   Some texts can be quite opaque on first contact. It is sometimes useful to ask students to decide the literal meaning of lines and then to reassess meaning in the context of the scene being studied. This can lead into a discussion of the nature and function of subtext.

3   One of the first needs is to grasp the storyline and plot. Students can be asked to represent this in a variety of forms, including written, diagrammatic or pictorial. It can be advantageous to represent the plot in physical shape, as shown in Figure 6.2.

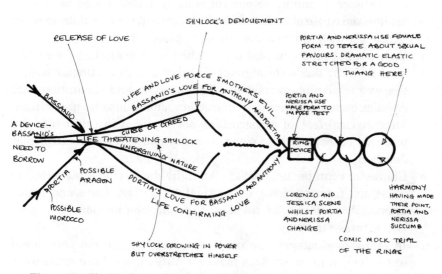

Figure 6.2 *The Merchant of Venice* – a plot diagram

The diagram form requires the student to decide on the relative importance of plot and sub-plot lines, the crucial dramatic points of shift between states in the drama and the overall dynamic form of the play. It can also chart the development of individual characters, and their relationship to each other and the plot. At their best such diagrams become a useful preparation for decisions on how particular scenes might be staged, as their physicality can give strong clues to appropriate dramatic form. With a suitable play, groups may be asked to represent the plot as a silent movie, with archetypal characters, music and a flicker light (see p.74). This exercise requires a thorough examination of the text to inform

85

decisions on the nature and relationship of characters, and the chronology of the play's events.

4 Once the skeletal form of a section of text has been decided, improvisation can be used to discover the dynamics of the drama, concentrating on key scenes which are nodal points in the total dramatic structure. Exploration of well-chosen sections often informs interpretation of other parts of the play. At first students use their own words in this enactment, gradually assimilating sections of the text. The aim is to experience the dynamics of the drama as embedded in the actions and reactions of the characters. Understanding may be enhanced by improvising scenes that do not actually appear in the text but that are suggested by hypothesis. In capturing a stage relationship that contains unexplained bitterness, for instance, it might be enlightening to improvise scenes which explore the cause of such feeling. Take care not to be sidetracked by improvisations which do not elucidate plot or characters.

5 Character studies are best approached by considering the motivation of individuals throughout the play and in particular within the extract being worked on. The liaisons and disunities that develop between individual characters should also be understood. The 'physical feel' of a character's development in relation to the plot can be explored by superimposing character lines on a plot diagram.

6 Characters can be 'hot-seated'. An individual actor is subjected to questions from students on motivation, intent, fears and aspirations. A variation is to have the questioning done by other characters in the play.

7 In many productions, the props and costume are not introduced until the last moment. This makes it difficult for these items to be fully integrated into the characters' stage behaviour. It is likely that very few of these materials will be needed or available in a workshop approach to a play not intended for widespread performance, as collecting them can be time-consuming and their use a distraction from the main task. The careful introduction of particular items, however, can be extremely useful in helping a student to find a character: a nervous character who constantly flicks the teeth of her *comb*; a threatening mobster who smacks the palm of his hand with a *beer bottle*; a woman in *black clothing* who continues to mourn; a melodramatic villain who enjoys floating his *cape* for effect.

8 Creative responses can aid a fuller understanding of the play:

- Copy a reporter might have filed after watching Mother

Courage, alone after the death of her children, harness herself to her cart and follow the armies;

- A news report at the scene of Willy Loman's car crash;

- Five telegrams sent by Willy Wonka from the chocolate factory;

- A report of Malcolm's succession from an eyewitness in Macbeth's castle;

- *Newsnight* from Illyria.

These exercises must be carefully chosen if they are to be more than mere distractions. They should take the students further into the text, not allow them to fantasize away from it.

Textual study workshops should encourage students to take intellectual risks in opening up the dramatic potential of a text. The drama undertaken should be viewed as work in progress, to which students can contribute in an atmosphere of mutual, positive criticism. In this way the teacher becomes a facilitator and guide, allowing students room to discover their own views within carefully organized lessons.

A practical approach

The words of a text are necessarily the starting point for any interpretation. Students need to consider a number of interpretive possibilities before they settle on one that can be used as a starting point for exploration.

To demonstrate the potential for different meanings, you can use a simple expression such as 'Mmmmmmmm!' This can be, depending upon the context and the feelings of the person saying it:

a suppressed scream;
a murmur of admiration;
dissent – if accompanied by a shaking of the head;
agreement – with a nodding of the head;
inspiration – if accompanied by a raising of the eyebrows;
a tune being hummed;
an imitation of a car engine;
an imitation of a fly;
an expression of frustration.

Try to give full voice and action in demonstration of these and similar possibilities; otherwise the exercise becomes a dry one. After each, ask the students to identify what the character is expressing.

Discussion of differing interpretations of this simple bit of text should reveal the concept of *meaning in context,* which requires the extract to be set within the scene and play as a whole before decisions can be made about which, if any, of the suggested interpretations is valid.

Having established the principle of interpretation, give groups of students identical pieces of very short text to work on. An example of such text might be:

> *You know you're not supposed to be here.*
> *Do you mind?*
> *Gold, pure gold.*
> *Give it here!*
> *Catch me if you can.*

Stage directions and names of characters are deliberately excluded. The groups must work out the 'base of the iceberg' on which these speeches rest. Remind them that one line does not necessarily follow immediately on another and that the drama can be carried in action without words for considerable periods.

Two possible interpretations of this text which groups might arrive at are:

[A] Setting – a Hollywood 'corn' movie set.

Characters – a man and a woman with heavy American accents – lovers.

The cameras are rolling, the director's finger-snap signals the actors to start.

The woman is sitting on a stool in front of a mirror, doing her hair. The man enters behind her and kisses her on the back of the head. She looks up at him and says:

'*You know you're not supposed to be here.*'

The man starts to lift her hair, disturbing the grooming. She, playfully, says:

'*Do you mind?*'

He continues to let the hair fall through his hands, saying:

'*Gold, pure gold.*'

He removes a comb from her hair. She, playful again, turns on the stool and exclaims:

'*Give it here!*'

He retreats behind the bed and calls provocatively and invitingly:

'*Catch me if you can.*'

88

[B] Setting – a badly lit cellar.

Characters – four thieves who are tipping out the spoils of a raid on to a crate around which they are gathered.

Silently and with obvious authority, the 'boss' is dividing up the jewellery, with double shares for himself. No one dissents.

Suddenly they become aware of a figure watching them from the doorway. The boss tells the newcomer:

'You know you're not supposed to be here.'

Tension develops as the intruder walks slowly to the table. After looking around the group, all of whom, except the boss, drop their eyes, he picks up the most valuable piece of jewellery. The boss, feeling his authority threatened, speaks sharply:

'Do you mind?'

The intruder faces him down and, swinging the piece of jewellery in the boss's face, says menacingly:

'Gold, pure gold.' (subtext here, for he is not just referring to the jewellery, but to his own value too)

He walks backwards towards the door and pauses on the threshold, looking at the others. The sidekicks look at their boss to see what he will do. He rises and holds out his hand. The intruder does not move. After a pause, with the others judging his ability to handle the challenge to his authority, the boss says:

'Give it here!'

Again a pause, then the intruder places the jewellery in his pocket, defiantly. He leaves his hand in that pocket. The boss makes a move towards him, but as he does so, the intruder's pocket distorts to the shape of a gun. The boss stops in his tracks. Taking his hand from his pocket for the ostentatious removal of a piece of fluff from his jacket, the intruder says brazenly:

'Catch me if you can.'

He turns and goes out of the door. The boss makes no effort to go after him. He has lost this trial of strength and his authority over his sidekicks is severely dented: evidenced by their sardonic smiles when he sits down, and the loot's redistribution by one of his sidekicks – in equal shares.

Both examples are melodramatic and of little lasting dramatic merit, but they illustrate how the same piece of text can be different things in different contexts, as well as highlighting the importance of use of space and actions. Given five or six differing interpretations of identical text within the same class, the basic principles of interpretation are easily noted. These exercises may be referred to when more sophisticated texts are being dealt with.

For most purposes, the piece of text being considered must be short. Teachers must have realistic expectations regarding how many lines students can be expected to learn and work on. The enactment of five lines in interpretation B above could last three or four minutes and the real tension of the drama between boss and intruder could be lost if actors are holding, and constantly referring to, pieces of paper. Students dealing with excessively long chunks of text can, through efforts to 'get to the end', miss crucial non-verbal interaction within the scene.

Shortened text

The enactment of isolated scenes from a play may be given plot context and continuity by narrated or acted links. The narrator carries the story from the end of one scene to the next:

> *So that was the problem; Mary just didn't trust him and she decided to tell her friends about her problems. Well, inevitably Mark found out and later that evening he confronted her.*

Characters may step out of the play to provide first-person commentary:

> *After that I felt alone, quite isolated and a bit defensive. I thought about it for ages, and we had several rows, one big one in front of my parents. After a few days I couldn't take any more of the infighting, so when I saw him looking through the photographs I thought I would try and apologize.*

Such links bring coherence to the study of isolated moments from the play. A whole text can be dealt with by allotting important extracts to groups within a class, then linking them together in the manner described.

Shakespeare

In their efforts to 'study' his plays, students sometimes forget that Shakespeare was a jobbing playwright and actor and all his plays were intended for performance, not the systematic, desk-bound deconstruction they currently so often attract. The value of textual study through enactment is particularly important here if our charges are to stop seeing his work as merely puzzles to be solved.

Shakespeare's plays can provide particular problems due to their unfamiliar syntax and vocabulary. Even when the literal meaning of lines is grasped, Shakespeare's rich use of metaphor often requires a further search to discover a character's true expressive intention. His lines can seem an unfathomable riddle to inexperienced students so it is advisable to work on very short sections in which the dramatic structure and motivations of the characters are most easily discerned. Older students should be introduced to verse-speaking. It is essential that the plot be understood quite quickly, giving the sense of the good story which is embedded in all Shakespeare's works. Once initial difficulties have been overcome, there is much pleasure to be gained from the unique dramatic possibilities that Shakespeare offers, and as study of his plays is now compulsory in state secondary schools at Key Stage 3 for Level 3 upwards, with the English order specifying the study and testing of three particular plays, teachers of drama may have much to contribute in this area.

Once a section has been chosen, students should work out the literal meaning of the script, referring to the footnotes in a good edition such as the Arden Shakespeare. They should then look at the meaning in context, discussing and recording the dynamics of character motivation and relationship. With younger or less experienced students, it may be worth setting up improvisations to explore these areas, until a sound grasp of the extract's dramatic shape is achieved. The students' words can then be replaced by Shakespeare's. Encouragement should be given to students to speak the words with confidence and conviction, for once the rhythm and power of the language are discovered, students often display pleasure in expressing it. Do not be afraid to cut some of the more obscure language, especially classical references or allusions to people and events specific to Shakespeare's time.

The following well-known approaches are examples of 'ways into' Shakespeare:

- A short 'silent movie' is made of the entire story, complete with flicker wheel, appropriate captions and the portrayal of archetypes.
- A series of tableaux depict crucial moments in the story. Students view these for discussion and change their forms in the style of forum theatre.
- Different groups portray the same section of a scene through different forms or genres – puppets, silent mime, movement, radio drama, soap opera, horror movie or melodrama, for instance. This enables them to discover and compare opinions on the dynamics of the piece without becoming bogged down in detail.
- One group of students prepares an extract for live performance while another creates the same piece in televisual format.

- In pairs, students prepare a ten-minute story that covers the main aspects of the plot. This is told to classmates or to another class which is about to tackle the play.
- Students compare their performance of a short extract with two contrasting video recordings of the play.
- In pairs, students decide how they would direct a scene – the blinding of Gloucester, for example – then compare it with videoed versions of the play.
- Students work out a fight or battle sequence as a focal point for the study of a scene – Macduff's killing of Macbeth, for instance.

Secondary students can be highly motivated by preparing a shortened performance of a play for presentation to a younger audience, perhaps a local primary school.

The 'Shakespeare in Schools' project, directed by Rex Gibson, has done a lot to improve the teaching of the plays. Local education authorities are also producing material for guidance and much of it relies upon an English/drama approach (see, for example, Jones *et al.*, 1993).

Suitable plays

Often in the secondary school, drama may be taught to a class by the member of staff who teaches it English and this facilitates cross-subject use of dramatic texts. Where this does not happen, drama teachers may choose to relate their work on script to the plays being dealt with by their colleagues who teach English. Where free choice is possible, teachers should be careful to select plays accessible and interesting to the age-group that will work on them. Over the last decade there has been a considerable increase in material aimed at this aspect of the curriculum and teachers in all phases should have no difficulty in finding appropriate plays. Some are published with accompanying suggestions for workshop approaches to the play, together with background material to the issues carried in the text. The 'Plays Plus' series, published by HarperCollins, is a good example of the genre.

In all work on script, the aim must be to demystify the form, giving the students control over the material and the process by which it is transformed from words on the page to live drama. There is much to be gained at all age levels if the teacher can unlock the satisfying drama which is to be found in all good scripts, whether they be enduring classics such as the Theban plays, or an effective scene written by a primary school student.

Chapter 7

SHARING TO PERFORMANCE – THE
COMMUNICATION CONTINUUM

> Sometimes the most suitable way of conveying the knowledge pupils gain
> through drama is by showing it to others, for it is a feature of performed
> drama that it conveys meanings in a condensed and deliberate way to an
> audience. (HMI, 1989, p.8)

If we accept educational drama as a continuum, stretching from
structured play to public performance, then *ipso facto* we accept the
need for a variety of communicative forms within it. The different
facets of this communication must be understood if they are to be
placed appropriately. Almost always within lessons, the communication
concerns 'work in progress' and pupils should be encouraged to see it as
such. In the speculative and exploratory stages, most of the communication will be confined to each working group. Students will discuss
ideas amongst themselves and try out ideas in action, occasionally
talking to the teacher who moves around the groups to monitor and
support activity. At the end of the exploratory stage, students may
wish to communicate aspects of what has emerged. This is done in two
very obvious ways: through telling us about the drama and the issues
it carries, and by the use of the medium itself. These two forms are not
mutually exclusive and are often used in combination, for it is difficult
to divorce the message from the dramatic form in which it was
expressed. David Best goes so far as to say: 'to the extent that the
meaning can be expressed independently of the particular work of art,
that work is a failure' (Best, 1990, p.4).

It is necessary for students to understand why they are watching the
work of others and it is the teacher's responsibility to define and
inform them of the purpose. Much of this communication amounts to
the sharing of ideas between fellow and equal practitioners. Although
it has acquired some precious overtones, the term *sharing* usefully
marks out this form from performance. No formal audience need be
present as those who are receiving the drama can remain seated in
their own work area or, if this is impractical, sit informally on the floor
around the group which is sharing its work. This is the equivalent in
fine art terms of discussing sketches on a common theme.

A more sophisticated form of sharing takes place when groups have clearly defined and polished the distillation of understanding and meaning derived from a particular exploration. Here the group sharing its work may choose to heighten its sense of audience by the deliberate arrangement of observers. Using the art analogy again, this mirrors an in-group presentation of a finished artefact.

The teacher's role is important in both these forms of sharing. She must ensure that a trusting atmosphere is created where individuals and groups feel safe in sharing their thinking through action. Feedback should be given in a positive way – asking the group which is presenting its work to talk about it first can be a sound principle, with others contributing afterwards. This allows the sharers to identify the parts they feel best encapsulate the meaning they are after, although at first they may chiefly express that by describing which parts 'worked best'. It also allows them to relate which sections of the drama they are *not* so pleased with and to offer suggestions about how they could be improved. This can be a useful framework within which to invite observations from the rest of the class:

• What do you think worked well, and why?
• What was less effective and why?
• How could it be made *more* effective?

This structure rules out negative and destructive comment and the desire to see things as either 'good' or 'bad'. It is very natural in this ambience to ask groups to go away and act on points which emerge from the evaluative discussion:

> *So we are agreed then – we need to make the stylized parts much sharper and quite a lot shorter. Let's see if we can work on that for the rest of this lesson.*

> *All groups feel the action should stop while the toy-maker is waking, so can you discuss the changes you will need to make and try them out in your next run-through?*

At best the process described helps to develop a positive critical attitude to the medium as well as a sensitive awareness of the needs and rights of others in the drama class. It also exercises the crucial skills of making and reading effective dramatic metaphors.

It is important that the teacher does not monopolize the comment or constantly promote her own thinking to the detriment of that of the students. It is the teacher's responsibility to introduce the subject-specific vocabulary which allows the students to talk about the medium. The teacher must also protect the less socially, intellectually and dramatically able students from the unreasonable criticism of others.

If the group or the teacher detects a general weakness in the work during this sharing process, she should find the most appropriate way of strengthening it. This might be the teaching or heightening of a skill:

> *Let's do some concentrated work with the masks for twenty minutes.*

the provision of a supplementary dramatic experience:

> *If you are having difficulty feeling what it is like for the Incas to give all that gold to the Spaniards, let's try a similar improvisation set in your own time and culture. Let's imagine. . ..*

or a general exhortation to develop a much higher quality in the work in general, or in a specific area:

> *It's coming on, but the movement sequences are still too woolly. Cut away all the moves you don't need and pare it down to the bare minimum needed to show the journey. That's the challenge for the next fifteen minutes.*

If the teacher wishes to focus attention on one particular skill, concentrate on that as groups share their material, again using the 'doers speak first' principle. This allows the teacher to draw out selected teaching points embedded in the shared pieces:

> *If you had more time in that group, how would you work further on the narration?*

> *What do other people think about that?*

A useful way to extend in-class sharing is to invite parallel classes to share their work with each other. This can be especially effective if both classes have been working on the same topic. It can take place within lessons if there is sufficient curriculum flexibility, at lunchtime or after school when the 'out-of-lesson' timing can give an added significance and status to the work. The content need not be restricted to drama material. Other art forms, especially interpretations of the same topic in different media, and presentation of material from other curriculum areas can provide interesting collages of cross-curricular understandings of a topic. Thus a period of study on the building of Britain's canals could contain folk songs (music); illustrative art, including canal art (art); descriptions of the engineering process (technology); dramatization of some of the social impacts of the navvies on communities (drama); an explanation of the canal network (geography); an explanation of why the canals came to be built (history); readings from relevant literature (English).

The following examples demonstrate how a number of the communicative forms mentioned above work in practice. They show how students may operate at different points on the continuum within the same project, in this case an English and drama activity based on 'giants' carried out with an upper junior class.

Stage 1

Following a variety of work on the theme, including hearing and reading stories about giants and drama activity structured by the teacher, the class is divided into groups. Each group is invited to consider creating a dramatized story (a better term than 'play' at this stage, I think) about a particular giant. They may use elements of the work and stories they have covered so far, but the story will essentially be their own creation. The teacher discusses and makes explicit the story structure implicit in the stories they already know.

The groups begin work. In one group students discuss the structure of the story which they have decided to call 'Giants don't always win'. As they talk, they use their bodies and voices to demonstrate the dramatic form of some of their ideas. After trying out stilts, they reject them in favour of a distinctive voice and a way of moving to characterize the giant. One student shows the others how this might be done; another leaps up and demonstrates an alternative way of moving the legs. Here the students are shifting easily between talking about their intended use of the medium and using the medium itself as a vehicle for explanation.

Stage 2

After two lessons, the giant stories have been satisfactorily developed and shaped, and are now shared within the class. Each may be preceded by student introductions which address technical matters:

> *Rachel's away today, so Michael has to play two parts, so if you see him struggling to get out of the big coat, be patient.*

or provide a lead into the story:

*Our giant is called Pundi. She has always eaten cows and sheep –
any animal in fact which the frightened farmers have been silly
enough to put in the fields next to the mountain. But on this
particular day . . . well, let's see what happens.*

Each group's story is discussed, allowing those who present a story to
make first comment. Comment is encouraged from others with the
teacher saying:

What did you like about that?

or

What worked well in that story?

After a discussion of the most successful aspects the teacher asks the
sharing group:

*What would you want to work on and make more successful if you
had the time?*

Their replies are used to involve the rest of the class in a discussion on
how the drama could be strengthened.

Stage 3

The class decides it wants to show its stories to another class. The
teacher explains they are now moving into the realm of performance
and a decision is made to spend more time polishing up the stories on
the basis of the comments and decisions made after each previous
sharing. One or two students from each of the six groups meet with the
teacher at lunchtime to discuss the order in which the stories should be
performed.

Having decided to link the stories by narration, they discuss three
possible story orders and the kind of narration that might be used; the
order is suggested by chronology (how long ago the giant lived):

*The giant in our first story lived many millions of years ago when
ice covered the land. As it started to melt, Trizer, for that was the
giant's name, realized there would be a terrible flood, so. . . .*

or geography (how far away from Britain the giant lived):

*Our stories begin with a giant who lived many many years ago in a
cave where this school now stands. In fact if you listen carefully,
you may notice some names you recognize. . .*

or the cruel/kind nature of the giant involved:

> *We have all heard stories of nasty giants who tread on houses and eat people, but Bigsoftee – that's him over there collecting small sticks to help the birds who are nesting in his beard – wasn't like that at all. . .*

The students decide to accept the last structuring and during the next two lessons the stories are welded together into a complete statement which might now be called 'Our play about giants'. The students become sure of the running order and how all the links are made. Each group ends its story with a freeze-frame. Cassette music is faded in, fading down to background as the narrator provides the link to the next story. As the narrator speaks, the frozen group melts away and the next group takes up a frozen starting position. As each narration finishes, the music swells slightly before fading underneath the first action from the new group. Music control and narration are done by a range of individuals not involved in the action at that particular time. They work to a cue system:

> *The music comes in as soon as the giant says 'I'm sorry'.*

> *The mother can come out of freeze to stroke the dog when the narrator has said, 'But imagine what it must be like to have a fifteen-foot-tall daughter'.*

The running order, cues and names of students handling aspects of the performance are displayed on a large, clearly visible sheet.

When the play is ready it is performed to the other class. Before it starts, some students explain briefly to the audience what stages they have gone through in creating the play.

Stage 4

The performance to the other class went so well that a decision has been made to perform the play for an outside audience. The class which had been audience in Example 3 is to provide live music to replace that previously played on cassette-recorder. Story groups are paired with parallel music groups and these paired groups discuss the style and placing of music within and at each end of the story. They also consider incorporating live sound effects made almost entirely by vocal and percussion sounds. Each group finds an area of the school where it can work undisturbed by the necessary noise of the others. Over several days, the two class teachers help students use the sound to the drama's best advantage. Students are encouraged to be aware of how the drama may change as the music is developed and integrated. Solid rehearsals are held to remould the stories into a whole performance. Simple lighting is added – a spot for the narrator; one on performance area A and another on performance area B.

The play starts with a blackout. In the darkness, huge giant roars are heard (produced by slowing down a recording of student voices). The roaring gives way to music and, in a while, a light comes up on a narrator who leads us into the first story. As the narrator's introduction ends, more music covers a lighting cross-fade between the narrator's spot and area A, which reveals the characters in the first story. At the end of this group's contribution, the light on them fades to music and comes up on a narrator who links to Story 2 which is performed in area B. Groups leave or enter an area in silence and in blackout. The play lasts for 40 minutes, but no student contributes more than 5 minutes to it.

Coffee and biscuits are served in an adjoining space which has been arranged with artwork on the theme, including giant puppet heads, stories written by the children, enlargements of the notation used by the musicians, displays of story-books about giants, and another describing real giants from the past and a large flowchart with photographs explaining how the play was made.

A wide performance base

> We understand drama to be generically a performing art; performance, in other words, is as necessary and appropriate a part of drama as it is of music and dance. Given the right circumstances, we believe that children of all ages rise to the challenge of performance. On the other hand, without the presence of this performance element, children's work can sometimes become stale and repetitive. (ACGB, 1990, p.7)

Performance work can take many forms. As shown in the 'giant' project it can, and in many cases should, be seen as a natural extension of educational drama, not a bolt-on extra. Having got used to in-class and between-class sharing, mixed arts events held at lunchtime or immediately after school are a logical next step. The programme might include students' lesson output – polished improvisations, musical pieces, exhibitions of sculpture, paintings or technology pieces. Each contribution lasts no more than about 5 minutes, six items giving a programme length of about 40 minutes. Staff and outsiders might be encouraged to take part – folk singers, storytellers, instrumentalists, gymnasts and poets – to create an atmosphere of exciting endeavour. My most adventurous inclusion in such an event was a knife-thrower who threw flaming axes at the headmaster spreadeagled against a board. The audience loved it! Primary schools might seek contributions from staff and pupils at the local secondary school, secondary schools from a sixth-form college, higher education establishment, or their feeder schools. A typical programme in a secondary school could be:

- two numbers played by the school jazz band;
- a trampolining exhibition by Year 8 students;
- a dance piece from top juniors who will be coming to the school in September;
- a music student playing a computer composition;
- several Year 9 students exhibiting and talking about the collective collage produced by their class;
- a melodrama by a GCSE drama group;
- five minutes of magic by a teacher;
- a performance by a bagpipe-playing parent.

and in a primary school:

- Year 3 children sing a reaping song while others mime harvesting;
- a parent gives a display of computer artwork;
- Year 6 students play two tunes on the 'bottles-of-water band' they have made;
- two Year 7 students from the local secondary school read poems they have written on the theme of 'going up to the big school';
- Year 4 students, accompanied by the music of others, dance a 'bonfire and fireworks' dance.

Once the school is used to such mixed-arts events, thematic parties can be held at appropriate times in the school calendar – a Victorian evening with décor, costume, food and entertainment to match, for example.

Within this active and 'can do' climate, drama is seen as a vital part of the school's arts offering, as well as a contributor to the rituals and celebrations of the more general life of the school. With such a wide drama base, productions should emerge which would gain from an outside audience. The cross-curricular drama project described in Chapter 10 is an all-embracing example. These performance pieces are firmly based within the curriculum rather than being extra to it, and the teacher of drama can offer them with integrity to a wide audience in the guise of 'the school play'. Because they are embedded in the curriculum, the students have taken a full part in their development, and their familiarity with and ownership of the material usually leads to very effective performances. I recently watched a small village school perform a play based on the history of their community. A scene dealing with recruitment for the First World War, the family farewells, the fighting, the injuries and the deaths culminated in a poem spoken over the projected image of the village war memorial. Some of the clearly visible surnames of the dead matched those of their relatives in the audience. It was one of the most moving theatrical moments I have ever witnessed, and, more importantly, the performers felt its significance too.

If students experience the development, writing, directing and performance of their own scripts as explained in the previous chapter, they should be able to progress with confidence to handle plays written by others. Plays must be carefully selected to suit the age-group concerned, and rehearsal approaches should not conflict with the techniques familiar in educational drama. Some of the approaches described in Chapters 3 and 6 should be helpful in this respect. Many plays are naturalistic and involve adult characters. Even if they are being acted by older secondary students, decisions will have to be made about conventions that will allow youngsters to play characters much older than themselves.

Performance can be used as a meeting ground for school exchanges. I have taken young people to Czechoslovakia to perform, and our play provided the shared experience that enabled us to get close to our hosts in spite of the language difficulties. One of the most exciting projects I ever undertook involved the preparation of a puppet play and a movement performance in a school in rural Buckinghamshire. We performed these in a Yorkshire pit village over a three-day stay, supplementing them with joint workshops for visitors and hosts. The Yorkshire youngsters then brought a play to Buckinghamshire. We gained tremendous insights from staying in each other's homes, and the drama gave us the reason for doing it.

Teachers of drama in a particular phase of education should be aware of and liaise with organizations that provide additional drama experience for students who wish to do more. Youth theatres, drama clubs and societies and residential courses are available in most areas and where they are not, teachers should explore initiatives to bring them into being.

The majority of teachers of drama now see performance as an integral part of their teaching. It is clearly impossible to expect a 'school play' to be performed every term, but if sharing and performance are seen to be connected in the ways I have described, something from the drama canon will be communicated to an audience of some form at almost all points in the school year. Richard Fox, evaluator of the Exwick Project described in Chapter 10, states:

> So far as drama in the service of English is concerned, performances are not necessary or even desirable in all instances. The process of improvisation is more important than the product of performance. However it is worth noting some of the gains which came from the challenge of performance in this case. There is no doubt that the prospect of playing before an audience, or recording for a professional radio broadcast, lent status and a strong motivation to the work –
>
> 'As it grew closer to the performance, I got excited because we were actually showing a performance and acting towards our project on Victorians.'
>
> Performance brings with it acute anxiety –
>
> 'My legs felt like spaghetti.'
>
> but also a feeling of team spirit and responsibility. This may be felt towards others –
>
> 'I felt I had a responsibility over my whole scene because if I laughed, everyone would laugh.'
>
> or towards the self –
>
> 'I knew I had to do it right and if I didn't, I would not be happy with myself.'
>
> 'I thought the play was brilliant and now I'm not afraid to be in any other big play.'
>
> 'At school everyone was saying how good I was which made me feel dead pleased.' (Fox, 1990)

Chapter 8

DRAMA AND OTHER SUBJECTS

In this chapter each of the foundation and core subjects is considered separately. Treating them as discrete entities makes it easier to highlight their relationships with drama, although in practice they could, and in the primary school would, merge within projects and topics to give students a coherent experience. I am aware that in both secondary and primary sectors drama may have very close links with the other arts and English, but these special relationships are well known and are not acknowledged here in order to preserve clarity.

Though drama has its own form and language, its content must derive from elsewhere. This allows it, in all the many different forms in which it exists in schools, to relate naturally and productively to other subjects. In the secondary school, co-operation between subject specialists and drama staff requires a flexible approach on both sides. Drama lesson content may focus on agreed topics which can be prepared for, paralleled or followed up in the classroom. An added benefit is gained if the subject specialist can be present during the drama lessons. Alternatively, the drama specialist might be available when the classroom subject is taught. Often, owing to staffing and timetable constraints, this is only achievable by merging two classes. Whatever the form of liaison, discussions need to take place well in advance of the lessons so that high-quality, productive experiences can be planned. One of the most exciting outcomes of such teaching is the way initial, sometimes limited, teacher perceptions of what can be done are extended and deepened through professional liaison.

The National Curriculum documents urge teachers to consider this kind of co-operation. In secondary schools, the science document states:

> If the technique of handling drama in the classroom is unfamiliar to science teachers they will be well advised to seek collaboration with colleagues in the English or drama departments. (NCC, 1989b, F3, 2.4)

HMI recommends that all primary teachers see the teaching of drama as an inescapable part of their job, allowing drama approaches to pervade the primary student experience:

> The task for all primary school teachers, and particularly the teacher who takes responsibility for drama, is to see that opportunities for children to

develop dramatic concepts, knowledge, imagination, skills and attitudes are woven into the general experience of the curriculum. (HMI, 1989, p.15)

The NCC has issued a poster which

identifies references to drama in the Orders for English, science, technology and history and in the proposals for modern foreign languages. (NCC, 1991a)

Whilst this provides useful, if limited, guidance in the absence of any more substantial statement, it in no way indicates the range of possibilities for drama's contribution to the wider curriculum. This chapter gives more comprehensive guidance on this matter. Teachers must clearly identify their aims in using drama, and should evaluate its effectiveness in achieving those aims. If this is not done, drama may be judged as a dispensable extra rather than a central and vital part of the curriculum in all National Curriculum subjects.

The National Curriculum allows teachers to see what should be covered within each subject. Teachers should look at the subject attainment targets and programmes of study to see where they touch or overlap. Primary school teachers will have a detailed knowledge of all subject requirements and the application of such a comprehensive overview could result in truly integrated topic work.

In the explanations which follow, examples as well as actual programmes of study are given. This is because the examples sometimes give a much clearer model of what students might *do* in lessons. The suggestions for the use of drama in no way constitute an exhaustive list. Teachers should view them solely as models of how drama might make a contribution in all areas of the curriculum.

Drama and English

Planning for drama in the classroom requires a clear understanding of its nature and the contribution it can make to children's learning. Drama is not simply confined to one strand in the statements of attainment which ceases after level 6. It is central in developing all major aspects of English. (NCC, 1990a)

In many secondary schools, drama emerged from English departments in the 1960s to become a subject in its own right. With the coming of the National Curriculum, it has been placed firmly back in the English domain. Many drama teachers see this as a retrograde step, but it does give drama, as the quotation above implies, a major place within a core subject, and should not preclude it making close relationships with other areas of the curriculum, as Chapter 10 attempts to demonstrate.

In the integrated curriculum of the primary school, the debate about where drama is to be placed is of little relevance as it can, and should, permeate the whole curriculum. In secondary schools it is likely that specialist drama teachers will endure, and though there may be a slow drift to drama taught by English staff, most would still prefer a specialist to be on hand to teach and advise on the body of skills which are essential for the effective use of the medium. Teachers of English and drama should liaise closely on how their subjects can co-operate to the benefit of all.

The English documents are peppered with suggestions for the use of drama techniques. The Non-Statutory Guidance lists particular approaches (NCC, 1989a; NCC, 1990a, 3.11), all of which are covered elsewhere in this book.

The documents consider drama within English to be of three types:

1   Drama as method
2   Drama as communication
3   Drama as text (NCC, 1990a, 3.0)

Drama as method

> As a 'learning tool', drama can make a contribution to all of the attainment targets in English and to other subjects. (ibid., 3.2)

The purpose of much of this book is to show how drama can do just this. It is clear, on the evidence of the respective subject documents, that the contribution is a major one and teachers who do not employ it will place unnecessary restrictions on the range of approaches available to them.

Drama as communication

> Through the programme of study, pupils should encounter a range of situations, audiences and activities which are designed to develop their competence, precision and confidence in speaking and listening. (ibid., POS, AT1, 2)

Drama provides varied contexts for language use. If a secondary teacher wishes to look at polemic, officialese, the language of compassion, debate or persuasion, dramatic situations can be devised to suit. Drama can create the laboratory in which students experience and observe characters who employ the words and forms under study.

105

The primary teacher will find opportunities to vary home-corner play situations, being able to modify the location and pattern of language use quite easily. Changing a few key artefacts and providing simple costume should be enough to suggest a sense of changed place. The principal use of the drama will be to place students in 'other people's shoes' so that they may experience differing language demands. The English document states:

> Teaching at this level [10] should make more explicit what has been previously noted incidentally, ie how language can be a bond between members of a group, a symbol of national pride, a barrier and a source of misunderstandings, and can be used to insult, wound, offend, praise or flatter, be polite or rude. (ibid., 21)

Each of these language functions can be studied in dramatic context. Drama concentrates on speaking and action, the predominant language modes of daily life. It can, however, relate strongly to written form. One example mentioned frequently in the documents is writing in role, an approach which enables students to use registers appropriate to particular audiences.

This is a logical extension of drama work, and involves developing characters within the drama who subsequently communicate in writing – pirates who send a ransom note; residents, who fear that planning blight will result from industrial development near their homes, writing to the local council; doctors in the year 2050 engaged in spare-part surgery writing an ethical code. Sometimes the writing in role might precede the drama. It is quite possible for it to be done in the classroom following drama experience and then be used to energize the next drama lesson – the pirates have captured the rich princess in lesson 1. In the classroom, students in role as pirates write a ransom note and devise a map of the island where the princess is held captive. Officials devise a letter to all pirates laying out the law and punishments available to the courts, whilst the royal family draft a general letter appealing for help in finding their daughter. In the next drama lesson, these documents, previously unseen by the groups to whom they are addressed, are delivered and the drama progresses. The English documents recognize this role:

> Drama can provide a way of extending the range of audiences, by writing within a role-play or simulation. (ibid., AT3, B7)

Students must come to realize how improvisation works, and how it can be set up. Such knowledge should lead to a state of autonomy where drama techniques take their place among other exploratory and expressive approaches. NCC English acknowledges this:

Pupils should be given the opportunity to learn how to use, and understand the use of, role-play in teaching and learning. (ibid., POS, AT1,6)

It is essential that the basic principles of improvisation are understood and applied (see Chapter 3), for without focus and tension the role-play exercises may be sterile.

Students need not show or share their work for 'drama as communication' to take place. The very act of sustaining a spoken role within a scene leads to the practice of a very rigorous form of communication, where the unpredictable and reflexive nature of the dramatic medium draws responses from the participants. Teachers should know their reasons for inviting students to share work and should not fall into the habit of expecting everything to be so treated.

Communication can take place within the medium or through demonstration and explanation:

> *Tell us what were the main points to emerge in your scene, Sarah. How do you think the pirates will react to that kind of letter?*

Often the two modes will be combined, as when students share four freeze-frames showing the main stages of a character's development while a group member points out the subtleties of what is depicted and the experiences that engender the changes.

Drama as text

Pupils should approach plays throughout the dramatic medium; children should often see or participate in the play being acted and not just read the text. (ibid., D11, 3.4)

It is clear that drama has a major part to play in bringing text alive. Although some teachers believe dramatic texts can be, and often through necessity are, studied without being dramatized, realization in action is preferable. In the same way that musical notation is for playing, scripts are for performance. The purpose of the drama must be clearly understood. It is usually employed to:

- illuminate or hypothesize on some aspect of plot, character or motivation, by bringing the characters alive in situations from within and outside the plot: or
- develop an appreciation of the differences between literary and dramatic forms.

Appreciation of text in action can be achieved by watching a recording of a performance – there is much to be gained from showing contrasting interpretations in extracts from different productions – seeing a live performance, or acting out sections of the text. Students should not work on too many lines, or they will almost certainly skate over the meanings embedded in the words in the rush to get something together. It is virtually impossible to develop believable characters and relationships while holding scripts. Short extracts can be learnt between lessons so that scripts can be dispensed with. A thorough study of manageable extracts can help students unlock a play's meaning, passing to them the onus of getting to grips with the text. The teacher's role is to build this practical experience into a planned exposure to the play, leading students to a sound knowledge of plot, dramatic form and character. Above all, the teacher's role is to ensure the pupils are intrigued by the issues carried within the drama, and in this the students' 'feeling responses' can be greatly informed by the practical work. Detailed guidance on approaches to text are given in Chapter 6.

Plays will not be the only texts to be worked on through drama. Poems, short stories and novels can be fertile starting points for dramatic activity, although teachers must be clear in their aims and aware of the difficulties in turning literature into drama, lest a pallid copy of the original emerge. The task of adapting part of a novel or short story to the dramatic medium can be fascinating. Showing a video of an adapted story the students have read – *Charlie and the Chocolate Factory; The French Lieutenant's Woman; Silas Marner* – provides a useful spur to discussion on the differing qualities of the two media.

Unless there is some good reason not to, all such drama should be informed by a close study of the text. Students may deviate from the 'truth' of the text to experiment with its characters and plot – what would have happened if Shylock had shown some compassion in court? What would Scout have said to Boo if she had met him by the message tree? These techniques can make more manifest the moral and social world the characters inhabit. Characters from the storyline can be hot-seated. Questioning minor or invented characters can be useful – what does the doctor or porter make of the incidents at Macbeth's castle? How did Willy Loman's condition appear to the family physician? What does 'the foul witch Sycorax' think of Prospero's release of Ariel? What does the straw-carrier think of the three little pigs' attempts to keep the wolf out? What does Miss Phelps the Librarian think of Matilda? The object is to give the students greater insight into the text, and the exercises must be carefully chosen and used in order to achieve this.

The public inquiry mode can be useful. This can be retrospective – a coroner's court following Willy Loman's death – or placed within the storyline – a case conference to discuss the rightful parent of Grusha's baby prior to Azdak's court findings.

Media reports which involve speculation and invention based on a sound knowledge of the text can allow students to extend, manipulate and juxtapose that knowledge – a radio interview with the riding-school owner in *Equus* following the blinding of his horses; a newspaper report on the one child left behind in Hamelin after the mountain closed. This kind of work has obvious links with media education (ibid., D16, 4).

Dramatic monologues of the Alan Bennett *Talking Heads* variety can provide an exciting challenge to students. It is a natural extension of character development and hot-seating exercises. Such monologues should be based on a developing understanding of the text, though they may contain elements of interpretation by individual students. Sufficient time and support must be given for these pieces to be created.

Appreciation of characters' attitudes in key moments of a text can aid an appreciation of the whole storyline. Tableaux can be formed to represent particular moments in plays and other literature. This can be an interesting way into text, as visualizations of crucial moments can be made quite quickly. A variation is to allow some students to arrange others who are in role in positions which represent the dynamic relationships of a scene. These concrete representations can be viewed and changed through discussion in the style of forum theatre, where students can adapt the tableau and question characters.

With the requirement to teach Shakespeare in English (ibid., POS, AT2, 15 and 24) teachers will find practical drama helpful in making the plays accessible. Advice on approaches to Shakespeare is given in Chapter 6.

Drama as subject

The above categories could be seen to exclude more complicated and sophisticated uses of drama. The English document recognizes drama's responsibility to enter the world of feelings:

> Drama also enables children to reconsider their feelings and attitudes in the light of shared experience. Drama provides a valuable way of learning about oneself and others. (ibid., 3.6)

It is likely that this function of drama will be addressed within drama as subject, taught in recognized timetabled sessions in both secondary and primary phases. It is there that the skills-base upon which successful drama rests will be taught, and the disparate student experiences which could result from constant cross-curricular co-operation are supplemented and allowed to cohere. Most drama teachers wish to co-operate from a base of subject strength, and although their subject may be helpful in delivering the agendas of other subjects, it has an agenda of its own, and this should be systematically addressed if dramatic activity in the widest sense is to flourish within our schools.

The stimulus response approaches outlined in Chapter 5 could be usefully employed in English, and Programmes of Study for Reading, number 14, specifically refers to this. Non-Statutory Guidance 4.0 relates English to media education, raising the possibility of using photographs described in Chapter 5. The relationship between drama and media studies is potentially a very strong one. *Taking photographs at KS1* shows how photography could be employed as an integral part of a drama programme, and other media texts such as television and radio programmes, films, videos, computer software, advertisements, newspapers and magazines have obvious links with drama (ibid., D19).

The documents provide the possibility of a triangular relationship between speaking and listening, reading and writing, and drama. Writing as a response to role play and role play as a response to reading involve a key role for drama.

Drama and science

The Non-Statutory Guidance for science points to a number of ways drama might contribute to the teaching of the subject. C16, 9.3 includes drama in the different ways in which students can communicate findings. E10, 6.5 mentions role play in exploring the different theories concerning continental drift.

F3, 2.4 specifically recommends drama approaches:

> When pupils act out incidents the experience can help them to remember and learn more effectively. It can also be useful for stimulating the different social conditions in which the scientific ideas arose, and motivate those pupils whose special talents are not those usually employed in Science lessons. Drama will probably not involve acting a set piece, or learning set lines; it is better when it includes a large measure of improvisation. (NCC, 1989b; NCC, 1990a, F3, 2.4)

A12-7.11 explicitly describes the drama way of working where pupils: 'divide into groups; agree upon individual responsibilities; decide upon objectives (what to do and how to do it); carry out the task; collect data; analyse and interpret; evaluate and draw conclusions; communicate to others'. This is a perfect match for the way human behaviour is examined through improvisation.

Let us take an actual example of drama being used. Christopher Joyce (1990) writes on how it will soon be possible to screen people for genetic diseases and predisposition to heart disease or cancer. Although there might be benefits – the more regular checking of individuals with a higher risk of contracting a particular complaint, for instance – obvious ethical and moral issues emerge. Such tests could group people according to genetic criteria – employers might wish to carry out genetic screening before taking someone on; partners may require a screening before getting married; insurance companies might charge higher premiums or refuse cover to someone more predisposed to illness, for example.

> In 1985, 49% of employers in the US required job applicants to take medical examinations. These ranged from psychological tests to X-rays of the lower back for construction workers. They included lie-detector tests, handwriting analysis and a broad array of psychological questionnaires which purport to tell whether a potential employee is honest, mature, well adjusted or productive. Employers are now testing employees' urine and sometimes their hair, looking for signs of drug abuse. (Joyce, 1990)

It is not unreasonable to posit that, if they became available, genetic tests would be used by employers.

This would be an ideal topic to explore through drama. Given that drama requires the construction of the detail of human circumstance, individuals could be placed in situations where moral dilemmas are explored and decisions made. This topic would probably work best with secondary pupils. A number of improvisations suggest themselves:

In pairs, A and B:

1   A is an employer who has selected B to take on a very important job. B is required to undergo genetic screening and during a meeting with A learns that the results are unsatisfactory. The tests do not show an imminent life-threatening disease, merely that B is predisposed to one. A is not prepared to take the risk, given the financial implications for the company if B should become unfit for work while in his/her employ. Both A and B are given the general information about the scene but only A is told the results of the test.

2   A is married to B. Before starting a family, they decide to undergo genetic screening. The results show that one of them carries a genetic formation which would give a 50/50 risk of any child being seriously malformed. A and B improvise the conversation which follows this discovery. To start the improvisation, the teacher role-plays a doctor who gives this information to all the couples collectively. At the end of the improvisation, the couples are questioned, in role, by the doctor.

Other areas of the science curriculum which could lend themselves to drama treatment are:

AT2, Level 3(b): Pupils should know that human activity may produce changes in the environment that can affect plants and animals.

This could be explored by setting up a situation based on the pollution of a river or the building of a new road, housing estate or airport. The extension of the M3 motorway through Twyford Down in Hampshire would be a suitable contemporary example. Students could either start from the Twyford Down evidence – press cuttings; ministerial statements; European Parliament directives; pressure-group arguments; biological surveys – and dramatize actual events from that case study, or the teacher could construct an imaginary case study, perhaps not to do with a motorway, then relate its processes and outcomes to Twyford Down. To ensure that the scientific content is accurate, students would need to research the nature of the environment and the harm that might be caused to it by development.

It is essential, as explained in the section on improvisation in Chapter 3 (see p.17) that the issue is not conceived as black and white. Not only will this be a misrepresentation of any case worth studying, but it will deprive the drama of its most valuable energy. Teachers should be careful to collect material to reflect both sides of the argument.

AT2, Level 10(c): Pupils should understand the basic principles of genetic engineering, selective breeding and cloning, and how these give rise to social and ethical issues.

Students could work in groups dealing with different aspects of these topics. Role cards could be used to give the exercise structure. Situations involved might be:

- a laboratory in which researchers producing chimeras by genetic manipulation of sheep and goat embryos have discovered how to do this with human and animal embryos;
- a discussion between doctors, a childless couple and a potential surrogate mother;

- a legal hearing where a divorcee mother's fight to have seven frozen embryos declared human life and not simply marital property is explored;
- a court scene where protagonists and scientists debate the status of 'orphaned' frozen embryos after the couple who supplied them were killed in a plane crash.

Students might extend the scientific study by speculating on future developments, based on a firm understanding of the scientific concepts involved. They should be given free choice to construct their own visionary models before sharing them with the class. Each group should be required to explain how their postulation relates to current scientific knowledge. Such speculation has a distinguished place in science. In this topic area, hypotheses concerning fish/human chimeras which can pierce enemy territory by underwater attack, artificial wombs and male childbearing have already been aired.

As in all drama work which deals with sensitive issues, the teacher should not plunder them as 'emotionally juicy topics'. It is essential that the reason for doing the improvisation is clear and that the lesson is structured and delivered in a way which avoids trivialization of the issues. It is important for the teacher to be aware of family backgrounds which could make the work unduly stressful for particular students.

The Non-Statutory Guidance points to other uses of drama. There is a suggestion that:

> Groups of pupils could be asked to represent families stricken by cholera. They would be expected to research the conditions and symptoms and then speak in character to the visiting doctor. After this, the class could make predictions about how cholera might have been transmitted and what further investigations should take place. (NCC, 1990a, F3, 2.4)

There is a danger that this could seem a neat little exercise to drop into a science lesson. If it is to work effectively, the participants must be given sufficient time to identify with the family structure. Teachers should refer to the details of the conditions required for good improvisation set out in Chapter 3.

A possible structure for an improvisation in this area might be as follows:

> *Pupils get into groups of five and are given role cards designating Smeech family members – father who works at the local workhouse where cholera is rife; mother who has a history of ill-health; daughter who has seen two of her friends go down with cholera; son who secretly still goes to see a friend in whose house there is*

cholera – even though his mother has banned him from doing so; a doctor who has decided, in spite of the danger, to see as many families as possible to warn them of the disease and to advise on precautions.

The situation is set in the Smeech family home, a one-bedroomed terraced house in a densely populated area. There is no bathroom or running water. Baths are taken in a tin bath in front of the open fire and water is fetched from a pump in the street. There is a communal toilet in a yard behind the houses, emptied once a week by a team who collect the night soil. Mrs Smeech earns extra money by washing clothes and bedlinen which her husband brings from the workhouse. They need this extra money to feed themselves and pay the rent. The daughter has left school and is about to start work as a maid at the workhouse manager's house. He will not employ her unless the doctor gives her a clean bill of health.

The time is 7.45 a.m. The family know that Dr Gooch is calling on each of the families in Brent Terrace in turn. Mrs Smeech has been up for some hours cleaning the house and making sure the family is as presentable as is possible given the poor circumstances in which they live.

The scene starts as Mrs Smeech is looking out of the window and sees Dr Gooch about to knock on the door. The rest of the family are sitting on chairs, Mr Smeech a little apart from the children. A chair has been set out for Dr Gooch.

The improvisation should last around six minutes with the doctor leaving when he hears the church clock strike eight – simulated by the teacher using a chime bar.

The doctor is given the special information that members of the families living on each side of the Smeechs have contacted cholera.

This improvisation assumes the class possesses some basic drama skills. Following the drama, pupils could:

1 carry out further research on the issues that emerged;
2 improvise a situation which follows the completed one;
3 write an individual account of what happens to the Smeech family in the following months. This could be done in a straight factual form or in an imaginative context – a newspaper story, for example;
4 discuss as a group what happens to the Smeech family following the scene depicted;
5 be provided with historical material which explains how cholera

was conquered in this country; how it remains in some other countries, parallel diseases; the principles of vaccination.

F3, 2.4 makes further reference to drama approaches:

> The replication of historical experiments, accompanied by a group argument about how the results should be interpreted, is another useful form of drama. (ibid.)

This kind of improvisation could fail unless the teacher is aware of the essential ingredients of dramatic structure. The context for the argument needs to be set up; the 'groups' who argue the different scientific standpoints must be identified and the individual characters within them developed.

A suitable framework might be as follows:

> *The king has set up an inquiry into arguments which have been raging. One instrument of that inquiry is to ask the two rival factions to present their case before a distinguished panel of three assessors appointed by His Majesty. Each faction is given time to present its case and to refute that of the other. Individual group members are drawn from different backgrounds – in Harvey's submission on blood circulation, butchers, vets, doctors with clinical experience and soothsayers might be called, for example. In a debate about the movement of the solar system, Galileo, a papal representative, other eminent astronomers, farmers (citing the effects of planetary movement on animals) and astrologers might be included. The teacher would need to research the various facets of the debate and ensure the pupils had sufficient factual information to work on.*
>
> *At the end of the hearing, the assessors could dismiss the 'non-factual' case but state that they are still not completely convinced by the 'factual' one. They request the group to go away and come back on a future occasion with evidence. This evidence could include actual demonstrations – showing the splitting of light for instance, or replicating the Reverend Doctor Joseph Priestley's demonstrations of the ingredients of air. The whole class could be split into groups to seek evidence, much of it demonstrable, that the new theories they espouse have validity.*

AT3, Level 8(c): Pupils should understand radioactivity and nuclear fission and the harmful and beneficial effects of ionising radiations.

This could be extended by setting up:

• a public inquiry on the siting of a new nuclear power station;

- an expert group addressing the general public on the need for a new radiotherapy machine at the local hospital;
- a debate about methods of disposing of nuclear waste.

> AT4, Level 9(b): Pupils should be able to evaluate the economic, environmental and social benefits of different energy sources.

This could involve a public inquiry where all the available energy generation forms are represented. This exercise is specifically mentioned at F3, 2.4:

> Simulation and role-play is a third kind of drama which is particularly useful for examining the scientific, economic, social and cultural aspects of technological decision making. Carrying out a role play debate about what kind of power station to build . . . will introduce economic and social issues. If the location is a Third World country an interesting multicultural element will also be involved.

This approach could be further employed at AT3, Level 9(d):

> pupils should be able to use scientific information from a variety of sources to evaluate the social, economic, health and safety and environmental factors associated with a major manufacturing process.

The drama might be enlivened by the presence of actual experts – radiographer, Greenpeace scientist, representative of Nuclear Electric – whom the students question in role.

Drama and mathematics

> The experiences of young children do not come in separate packages with 'subject labels'; as children explore the world around them, mathematical experiences present themselves alongside others. The teacher needs therefore to seek opportunities for drawing mathematical experience out of a wide range of children's activities. (Cockcroft *et al.*, 1982, para. 325)

The secondary curriculum offers little chance to relate drama and mathematics, although I expect enterprising teachers have been doing it for years!

The Non-Statutory Guidance states at F1, 1.6:

> Mathematics is a powerful tool with great relevance to the real world. For this to be appreciated by pupils they must have direct experience of using mathematics in a wide range of contexts throughout the curriculum.

Practical exercises to do with drama productions – measuring and scales in set design and staging, and co-ordinates related to audience seating – can be devised, and historical controversy concerning mathematical theorists – Malthus's population growth theories for instance, with attendant work on mathematical progression – could form the basis of useful collaboration.

It is in the primary school that the greatest potential for integration exists. The home corner can accommodate role plays with number work embedded in them, and many of the exercises involving collecting and sorting could be done in role. A market could be held, involving farmers, growers, stall-holders and customers, selling vegetables and fruit made in craft lessons. The guide-lines in Chapter 3 (see p. 17) on dramatic tension indicate how conflict could be introduced – following an accusation of sharp practice, the Queen's weights and measures officers require everyone to measure and weigh their products; the Queen will take away the stall-holders' rights if they cannot calculate her weight in cauliflowers.

In a drama based on the challenges used by a king to find those subjects who should inherit his wealth, a set of mathematical problems might be set. These might include a puzzle; designing a maze to a set of criteria; doing a probability test; measuring the weight and height of the king's subjects and producing a graph; finding out how to weigh the king's golden model elephant (Archimedes's theory of water displacement); making a royal staff with a perfectly shaped silver polygon at its head. These and similar activities give opportunities for teachers to work in role.

Interpretation of pattern and shape could be linked to movement work. One class could create the 'Land of Straight Lines and Corners', involving measuring, marking out and cutting small shapes for attachment to bodies as decoration or for placing on the floor to make patterns for the movement to flow through and around. Large-shape mobiles could be suspended above the area, and lantern barn-doors could give angular light pools on the floor. This could be contrasted with the work of another class in creating 'The Land of Circles and Curves'. Both approaches could embrace aspects of art – colour, texture, pattern; music – composing suitable sound for the movement quality; technology – materials, cutting and fixing; science – the colouring of light. Paired movement exercises could explore symmetry and asymmetry. Shadow drama could pose some interesting problems in calculating the size of shadow produced at varying positions between screen and light source and looking at concepts such as 'close to and far away' and 'enlargement and reduction'.

The mathematics documents place great emphasis on the communication of concepts and findings through the language of the subject. F1, 1.5 states that 'The overall aim must be to develop in pupils a positive attitude to mathematics, and an awareness of its power to communicate and explain' (ibid.). With this in mind, AT5, Level 2(a): 'pupils should be able to interpret relevant data which have been collected' (ibid.) could be extended in dramatic form. The two examples given in the document – collecting data on how students travel to school and birds visiting the bird table – could be handled in the normal way. The teacher might then place the class in role: children in a rural area meeting a council highways official to request more buses, a pavement and a safe dropping-off place; talking to a neighbour of the school who has demanded the removal of the bird table because the birds it attracts eat his soft fruit. The council official and neighbour could be played by teacher in role. Extension of the data collection into drama gives a social and political context for the work.

The Thomas Report of 1984 sought to encourage the application of mathematics in other parts of the curriculum:

> More opportunities should be taken than now to apply mathematical skills and ideas during the course of work that is not, principally, Mathematics. They may occur during the study of a topic . . . or a host of other activities. (Thomas, 1985, p. 34)

Such opportunities are not difficult to find and drama can play a useful part in providing the setting in which mathematical knowledge is used or its wider implications explored.

Drama and geography

Drama can be used within each of the five attainment targets, but its approaches are particularly relevant in Attainment Target (AT)4, Human Geography, and AT5, Environmental Geography, as these are laced with material on the ethical aspects of human responsibility for economic growth, and environmental care. Issues lending themselves to drama treatment can also be extracted from AT3, Physical Geography – different attitudes to the effects of coastal erosion is one example. The ethical debate which infuses much geographical study is presaged in Non-Statutory Guidance C25, where 6.9 states:

> Geographical enquiries are likely to give rise to debate about issues such as changing land use and pressure on natural resources. Encouraging pupils to consider opposing views, and different values and attitudes, can be helpful in promoting respect for diversity of opinion, an essential feature in a democratic society. (NCC, 1991b, p. C25)

and in 6.10

> Pupils should be encouraged to be aware of differing values and attitudes. A study of the growth of a settlement can be used to demonstrate how conflicts over the use of land can arise between: residents, employers, developers, conservationists, farmers and local and central government. (ibid.)

Drama activities are specifically mentioned in the documents, as in Non-Statutory Guidance C24, where role play and drama are listed as teaching methods. Role play is recommended in the sample of a unit of work on an environmental issue in C24: 'What effect has Kielder Water Scheme had on people, the economy and the environment?'

The conflicting priorities of environmental use are well in evidence. Section 6.10 recommends that pupils should be able to 'use knowledge of people's different viewpoints to predict the consequences of decisions', and gives an example of a focus for this: 'evaluation of proposals to establish a leisure centre in a green belt area'.

Dramatic approaches to such a topic could bear a close resemblance to the project on the youth club relocation described in Chapter 5.

The most obvious drama technique that might be used in geography is the public inquiry. This requires interest groups to research material required to convince a jury of their case. The jury could comprise classmates, another class, parents or other interested adults. One expanded example should suffice to explain this approach. The reader can extrapolate from this how similar attainment targets could be handled.

I will take the example given for AT5 6b: 'explain how conflicting demands can arise in areas of great scenic attraction', which is:

> analyse the conflicting demands in a National Park or areas of protected coastline or countryside, e.g. for farming, forestry, quarrying, military use, reservoirs, and recreational purposes. (ibid., p. 26)

This level of attainment should be met in the early years of the secondary school. The relevant curriculum work could be done before the teacher's announcement that the material would be used in an inquiry, but it would be much better to set this up from the start of the topic.

The teacher should choose an area of countryside which might conceivably be suitable for all the usages mentioned above. Interest would be added and fieldwork possible if the area were local. Small- and large-scale maps of the area, showing its relationship to the region and the country as a whole, as well as maps depicting the detail of the specific locality, would be required for each interest group. The teacher

119

might use press cuttings, articles and photographs about an actual case as introduction. Slides showing the progressive stages of a valley being flooded to create a reservoir, restricted access signs on a military training ground, the disfigurement of quarrying, the managed agricultural environment, an adventure centre and intensive forestation would be helpful in showing how landscape becomes transformed by human intervention. Such slides might include balancing material showing perceived benefits from various changes in use. If it is not possible for a visit to take place, a good teacher-produced video could be employed. This might include interviews with actual people or ones derived from role-play. Slides and video take time to produce, but they may be used again with other classes.

Each interest group would be provided with a pack of material giving essential contextual information, including settlement pattern, the reasons why their group needs to make use of the environmental resource, a geological map, specific information about their interest – factual and statistical – and a letter inviting them to present their case at a public inquiry. The information can be as comprehensive and detailed as the time available for the project and the age of the students allow. The teacher would act as facilitator, helping groups to find material relevant to their developing case. Cross-curricular links could be formed with art (the depiction of the area before and after), science (the analysis of different soils and rocks of the area), drama (the creation of a community which will be affected by any change of use), English (the writing of letters to MPs, councillors, newspapers; poems and creative writing on the environmental changes proposed – the first bulldozer blade cuts into the bark of a tree), technology (making a relief model), and most other areas of the curriculum. If two parallel classes were involved in similar projects using different locations and interest groups – one a rural location and the other urban, perhaps – they could come together to act as jury for each other.

In addition to the stated interest groups, others representing residents and environmental protection agencies could be introduced. If the area *were* local, evidence could be collected from actual residents. If it were not, evidence could be taken from communities that have been created within drama lessons.

Students must be clear about the nature of the task. The gathering of the groups' evidence and the form of the inquiry must reward an understanding of the principles of geography which underpin the exercise. The drama should not act as a cover for sloppy thinking, or be achieved at the expense of factual accuracy or geographical relevance. If the inquiry were held over two or three lessons, the groups would have an opportunity to discuss and develop counter-arguments to the cases presented by others. Time spent reflecting on the progress of the inquiry would be likely to deepen students' involvement and understanding. The process can be telescoped into two lessons if role cards are used, homeworks set, and out-of-lesson discussion between students encouraged and facilitated.

On the day of the inquiry, all participants need to be familiar with the procedure. The teacher could role-play the government-appointed inspector, or the post could be filled by a local planning officer or other suitable individual. The room should be arranged to give a sense of place and occasion, with technical aids such as overhead and slide projectors, flipcharts and display boards available. An air of seriousness and concentration should prevail, with all class members involved in the business of the inquiry in some way. Some participants might act as reporters, producing an article on the proceedings; others might video or photograph events. The topic could be the focus for several strands of related curriculum work.

The development and holding of the inquiry should be a significant event for the students. It is clear that it will take considerable lesson time to mount, and many teachers of geography may balk at this. It should be remembered, however, that the process can be referred to subsequently, when similar issues are being considered. In this way it will prove a valuable reference point for the students' learning. Because it may deliver attainment targets in other areas of the curriculum, speaking and listening in English for instance, it may be possible to plan the topic closely with other specialists. They may be prepared to use some of their lesson time to accommodate the project, thus lessening the sense of 'time loss' in geography.

This format, or adaptations of it, could be employed in considering a wide range of ATs in geography, especially those which centre on conflicting proposals for land use or decisions surrounding human impact on the environment. The following are some examples of alternative ways of working.

For AT4, 4c, 'explain the impact of recent or current changes in the place studied for 4b', the example given is:

> describe the possible effects on the settlement studied of proposals for a new housing estate in a village, or out of town offices or a supermarket in a suburban area. (ibid.)

Students could prepare a case for or against the development in groups representing the developers; residents for; residents against; local traders; planning officials; environmental protection groups. Each group comprising four or five students would be hot-seated by the others. Such work could form the basis of a primary school project.

In AT4, 4e: 'give reasons for the ways in which land is used, how conflict can arise because of competition over the use of land, and for the location of different types of economic activity', the example given is:

> consider the reasons for different views being held about proposals for a new road which would cut through an urban housing estate, or whether a particular rural area should be used for farming, forestry or as open space for recreational use. (ibid.)

Students prepare and share a variety of testimonies of people in some way related to the proposal. In the rural land-use issue, individuals could represent farmers, developers, walkers, golfers, other sports players, paint-ball combat enthusiasts, golf-course designers, foresters, wildlife experts, local councillors, planning officials, architects or Chamber of Trade representatives. A number of these individuals present their cases, none lasting more than five minutes. The teacher could use the material in different ways. Specific individuals could be brought together in discussion – a golfer, farmer and paint-ball enthusiast, for instance – while others watch. After several of the original talking heads have been heard, the class could decide which ones to call back for hot-seating.

In AT4, 5d: 'compare road and rail networks, and explain the effects of change to these networks', the example given is:

> examine the effect on people's lives resulting from the construction of by-passes; the introduction of one-way road systems; the closure of railway lines. (ibid.)

Students could research and role-play people from different eras who lived or live close to a road which has been progressively a village street carrying horse-drawn traffic; an upgraded road for early motor traffic; a widened road for fast traffic. Artwork depicting the road and conurbation development through the years is displayed as a time-line. Plans of the conurbation, as it developed in parallel with the road-widening described, are created. These are finally produced as overlays on an overhead projector for easier viewing. The conurbation now has the chance of being bypassed, and interest groups prepare their cases for presentation in role to another class.

In AT5, 4b: 'discuss whether some types of environment need special protection', the example given is:

> discuss the problems of protecting the habitats of rare species of wildlife or protecting a historic house. (ibid.)

Here the students might research how a wooded environment supports wildlife. They could choose one species – wood-louse, fox, squirrel, toad – and, through a personification of the creature, present a case showing how changes in the environment would affect its habitat and ability to survive.

There is considerable potential for developing performance work from geography topics. In AT3, 6g: 'describe some of the physical processes which can give rise to one type of natural hazard and how people respond to that hazard', the example given is:

> consider the conditions that produce river and coastal flooding, the circum-stances leading to a particular case of serious flooding and the consequences of the event. (ibid.)

Having visited Lynton and Lynmouth recently and seen the wealth of material in their Memorial Exhibition depicting the tragic results of the flash flood which hit those communities in August 1952, I could see how a cross-curriculum study of the flooding could become the focus for a major school production. Mini-presentations based on the episodic performance project pattern described in Chapter 7 (see p.97) may also be used.

Students could prepare a news broadcast dealing with a number of geographical problems around the world – the diversion of the River Danube in Slovakia, a tornado in the USA, drought in Africa, coastal erosion in Britain. Groups of students prepare a two-minute report which is fitted into a 'broadcast' lasting around fifteen minutes. Items are linked by two or more presenters and the whole is bracketed by appropriate music. A touch of reality may be achieved by the addition of a weather forecast. This format works well as a radio news feature: this can actually be recorded and either played to other classes or assemblies, or made available in a cassette-player for students to listen to individually. If the students are fired by the format, links with the local radio station may be possible. The news could be televised, with cuts to still pictures, interviews and reports from the scene.

In addition to the public inquiry approach, simple role plays in pairs and small groups can be employed. These are easily devised, and can be used in lessons without major organizational changes to the room or lesson format. Geography also offers possibilities for drama activity in cross-curricular theme teaching on environmental education and citizenship.

Drama and history

> Events are unfolded before our eyes. So it [drama] is a powerful way of bringing alive knowledge and experience which might otherwise be inert. (HMI, 1989, p.7)

Drama has a long and well-understood link with history. Much of the content of theatre unravels and speculates on the personalities, motives and effects of individuals and groups from the past, whilst history benefits from drama's ability to reconstruct the human detail that fleshes out the facts of past events. Practitioners and writers such as John Fines have demonstrated the benefits which can flow from the productive fusion of the two subjects (see Fines and Verrier, 1974).

In its Non-Statutory Guidance, the National Curriculum history document acknowledges links with drama:

> Drama can help pupils meet all history ATs. It can develop skills in communication and enquiry. It can help pupils understand the motives and behaviour of people in the past. (DES, 1991b, p.C11)

It recommends drama as a teaching method (ibid., C14) and form for communicating information (ibid., C17).

Drama approaches are often used in history to create empathy with the human beings involved in historical events. There has been a considerable argument between the 'facts' and 'empathy' factions over the content of the history National Curriculum. Teachers who value the empathy approach believe students will have a deeper understanding of the past if they can identify with the people who lived at that time.

> The ability to appreciate what it may have been like to be a particular person in a particular period of time is vital to an understanding of the past. (Woodhouse and Wilson, 1988, pp.10-14)

Opponents of empathy approaches believe that such work is no substitute for sound factual knowledge, and point to erroneous understandings of history caused by the creation of 'factional' dramas. Most teachers see empathy as a valuable teaching technique and ensure that any inaccurate dramatic reconstructions are compared with the facts as known. Often of course, we do not know all the facts, and it is the creation of hypotheses through drama which gives students the confidence to handle interpretation of evidence. The school log-book entries described in Chapter 10 are a good example, and the dramatic speculation on the cause of Edith Cornall's drowning (see p.167) shows how close students as historical detectives can come to the truth as subsequently revealed.

Drama activities would be of use in large numbers of the statements of attainment in history. In AT1, 1a: 'place in sequence events in a story about the past', in the example given: 'Retell the story of the Gunpowder Plot', the retelling could be in dramatic form. The public inquiry format described for geography could be employed in a number of areas. In example AT1, 3b for instance: 'give a reason for an historical event or development', the merits of canal and rail transport could be debated through the roles of rival engineers. AT1, 2a: 'place familiar objects in chronological order', would link very well with the drama approach to 'objects as stimuli' in Chapter 5. Local history studies could be integrated into the cross-curricular approaches described in the case study in Chapter 10. In each case, for the drama to be successful, the focus of and tension in the topics should be clear to the students.

Specifically, drama might be used in the following areas of history. For AT1, 9a: 'show an understanding of how causes, motives and consequences may be related', the history document gives the example:

> Present to the class an account of the causes of the Second World War, making connections between the consequences of the First World War, other general causes, and the intentions and motives of Hitler. (DES, 1991b, p.4)

The communication of material emerging during the historical study could form the basis for a drama collage presentation. Near the end of work on the topic, students could be asked to identify the significant events in the time-span being studied. When agreed, these should be organized into a time-line and drawn on a chart large enough for the group to see as an *aide-mémoire* of order and content. Individuals and groups should take responsibility for different aspects of the presentation, specializing in a particular part of the time-line, following lessons which acquaint them with the complete picture and give them access to appropriate research resources. The teacher would be responsible for setting the task in an interesting and challenging way, facilitating and guiding at appropriate points, and challenging the students' representation of events.

Such a collage presentation might include:

- *naturalistic monologues* – a Hitler speech; Chamberlain's declaration on his return from Munich; a statement from Marshall Petain;
- *reconstructions of actual events* – the Nazi invasion of Czechoslovakia and Poland;

125

- *tableaux and statues* – the sealing of the alliances between Germany and Italy, Britain and Poland. Large captions and speech bubbles could be used to indicate the main statements of the participants;
- *slides and photographs* – projected by episcope, made into acetates for the overhead projector, or projected on slides: Hitler, Stalin, U-boats, Churchill, Nazi rallies, Mussolini and Roosevelt, the Reichstag fire;
- *visual material* – charts, diagrams and cartoons;
- *contemporary recordings* – Churchill's speeches, radio programmes;
- *narration* – telling parts of the build-up not represented in other ways;
- *readings* – a contemporary newspaper account of Germany's annexation of Austria;
- *popular songs of the period* – live, and on tape – to link the units of material together.

The presentation should be based on sound historical material, with facts correctly represented. Where speculation is used to generate hypotheses, the outcomes should be based on an understanding of available evidence. Facts and opinions should be differentiated. The presentation should be evaluated by the teacher and students, with particular reference to its accuracy in depicting the actual causes of the war. This format could be developed into a full production.

For AT1, 9b: 'explain why individuals did not necessarily share the ideas and attitudes of the groups and societies to which they belonged', the history document gives the example:

> Give reasons why leading suffragettes differed in their views, from each other and from the social groups to which they belonged. (ibid., p.5)

This would be an ideal topic for hot-seating students in the roles of suffragettes and related characters. Detailed research into the people being played would be carried out beforehand. Simple costume could be worn. The students asking questions might be cast as police, parliamentarians, or other suffragettes. To create the necessary tension, the suffragettes might differ in their views on how the campaign should progress, following the death of Emily Davison, who threw herself under the King's horse on Derby day. Questioners could be other suffragettes, police, male Members of Parliament, women who disagree with women's suffrage or racehorse owners.

Hot-seating might also be used in the following attainment targets:

In AT1, 7c: 'show an awareness that different people's ideas and attitudes are often related to their circumstances' (ibid., p.4), the example given is:

> Show how economic hardship led some French people to support the Revolution of 1789.

Hot-seated characters and questioners could include Robespierre, the King on the eve of his execution, uncommitted peasants, royalists and revolutionaries, the man who operated the guillotine and someone who retrieved the silk handkerchief which bound the King's eyes.

In AT2, 2: 'show an awareness that different stories about the past can give different versions of what happened', the example given is:

> Detect differences in two adults' accounts of the same past event.

Here, two or more individuals caught up in the same event could be questioned – a factory-owner and someone involved in cottage industry during the Industrial Revolution; a parliamentarian and royalist being questioned about King Charles's trial and execution.

In AT1, 2c: 'identify differences between past and present times', the example given is:

> Talk about how life in a Viking village differed from town or village life today.

Such a study could form the basis of a reconstruction of Viking daily life. At this age, talk-through methods could be used to take students through experiences which have been understood by previous study. Family groups could then be formed, and the material for improvisation negotiated between teacher and pupils. When required, the teacher would guide the students on matters of historical accuracy, identifying areas of understanding that need further research before the next stage of the drama.

AT1, 3a asks students to 'describe changes over a period of time'. Their understanding could be enhanced by the creation of representations of scenes on related topics from different periods. In a rural area, this might focus on the changing nature of agriculture, and in a town on the development of public transport or the changes in a street over a period of time. The class could be split into groups, each depicting a stage in the time-line. Narration could be used as a linking mechanism. The work could be developed by individuals coming alive to speak their thoughts as the teacher touches them (see thought-tracking in Chapter 5, p.74). The concept could previously have been introduced by asking students to fill speech bubbles linked to characters in appropriate photographs. This work on photographs links closely with AT3, 1: 'communicate information acquired from an historical source'; AT3, 3: 'make deductions from historical sources'; and AT3, 4: 'put together information drawn from different historical sources'.

In AT1, 6c: 'describe the different ideas and attitudes of people in an historical situation', the example given is:

> Give a concise example of the range of views on the coming of the railways in Victorian Britain.

Work here could be enhanced by the holding of a debate on the motion 'This house believes that the railway is beneficial and here to stay'. Cases could be presented by a range of interested parties in role – railway navvies; railway engineer; farmer who will lose land; farmer and industrialist who welcome access to markets; vicar worried about the moral impact of the navvies and the increased access to the town on his parishioners; railway-owner. The participants could be members of a community which is being consulted about a new line, and at the end of the debate, when all points of view have been heard, the participants could be asked to vote for or against the building of the line. Actual examples of towns reluctant to accept lines – such as Eton, influenced by its school, and Oxford, by its university – could be used.

In AT3, 5: 'comment on the usefulness of an historical source by reference to its content, as evidence for a particular enquiry', the example given is:

> Talk about how information gained from a visit to an historic site can be used to reconstruct the way of life of its former inhabitants.

Following a visit to a stately home as part of a study of social history, students could reconstruct aspects of daily life in such a house. Better still, if the owner of the house was agreeable, the students might mount their reconstructions within it.

In the suggested supplementary study units (SSU), almost every suggestion of content given offers ideal contexts for drama activity. The following are examples in Key Stage 2:

> SSU 1, *Ships and seafarers*. The content could include ... living and working conditions on board ships.

The teacher prepares role cards for all class members covering the crew and passengers of a late seventeenth century ship. Five of the class are observers who conduct a 'fly-on-the-wall' examination of events. Five improvisations are run at the same time, each focusing on an aspect of shipboard life:

> The men complain to the captain about the poor food.
>
> The ship-owner, who is travelling as passenger, instructs the officers to work the men harder to get to port before a crucial deadline.

The cabin-boy complains of illness and the crew suspect smallpox.

A man falls from the rigging after being sent aloft in a storm.

Women passengers who are travelling to the 'New World' complain of bad behaviour towards them.

Assuming that the class has been introduced to the technique, the teacher uses forum theatre (see Chapter 5) to develop these and other scenes.

SSU 2, *Food and farming*. Villages and cities in the ancient world; the medieval village; nineteenth-century rural life; the impact of mechanisation and new methods of transport.

Following curriculum work about their rural community during the nineteenth century, a class of village-school students develop scenes in groups using original photographs as stimulus. When these polished, dramatized stories are shared, a slide of each photograph is projected on to a screen before a lighting cross-fade to the group members who are frozen in identical poses. As the music fades, the scenes come to life and are acted out.

SSU 3, *Houses and places of worship*. Domestic service and living conditions in houses: worship, festivals and ceremonies.

A woman who had worked in service watches scenes which students have developed around their curriculum study. She comments on each and tells of related events in her own working life.

SSU 4, *Writing and printing*. Censorship of written and printed materials; the effects of literacy on everyday life and work.

Using forum theatre, the teacher sets up an improvisation where a factory-owner in the 1860s interviews men and women who have applied for an overseer's job. One requirement of the job is that the person appointed should be able to keep a daily log of work done, and read material such as delivery notes and letters from suppliers.

SSU 5, *Land transport*. The impact of different methods of transport on the environment; importance of transport for work, trade and business; the effects of transport on society.

Using the youth club lesson model in Chapter 5, the teacher creates a community through the use of role cards. When that community is established, letters are delivered announcing that a motorway extension will run through or close to it. Residents hold a public meeting in the village hall at which representatives of the Department of Transport and the Campaign for the Protection of Rural England have been invited to speak. If necessary, the speakers' parts are taken by well-briefed older students or staff.

> SSU 6, *Domestic life, families and childhood* (all sections).

The teacher collects a number of objects from British domestic life at the turn of the last century – a dolly tub and dolly; a flat-iron; a moustache cup; a warming-pan; an oil lamp; a Dutch oven. After practice at creating stories from objects (see Chapter 5), the students in groups of five create a story on the lines of: 'This is no ordinary flat-iron/moustache cup. . .'

The Category B unit on local history on page F9 is a rich vein for drama work as well as being a perfect match for the cross-curricular project described in Chapter 10.

> SSU, *The Maya*. Gods and goddesses; creation myths; festivals, ceremonies and sacrifices.

Working from available evidence, students could create Mayan rituals. Additionally or alternatively, they could devise their own rituals to do with known Mayan celebration and compare their versions with the actual ones. The Mayan creation myths could be acted out and compared with some from other cultures.

> SSU 12, *Benin*. Everyday life; myths and folk tales.

Some students do a silent enactment of a folk tale while others narrate it to the rhythm of drums.

In Key Stage 3:

> SSU 1, *Castles and cathedrals 1066 to 1500*. The military, political and social functions of castles; cathedrals as communities.

Henry IV discusses with his Lords, castle-builders and Welsh spies the nature and positioning of castles on the Welsh Marches to resist the raids of Owain Glyndwr.

> SSU 3, *Culture and society in Ireland from early times to the beginning of the twentieth century*. The impact of English and Scots settlement on Irish economic and social life; religious divisions.

In pairs: A is an English settler who desperately needs help with a sick animal; B is an Irish person who has lost land to the incomers.

> SSU 6, *Britain and the Great War 1914 to 1918*. Changes in the role of women; changes in social attitudes.

In pairs, one boy and girl: A is a husband who has returned from the war and is disturbed to find how much things have changed; B, his wife, is a housewife and mother who worked in a munitions factory while he was away. She wants to get a job now the war is over. The husband resists.

> SSU 11, *The French Revolution and the Napoleonic era*. Society, wealth and poverty in France before the Revolution; problems of royal government before 1789; the ideals of the revolutionaries.

A group of revolutionaries try to convince a meeting of rather cowed and sceptical peasants that they would all be better off in a republic. During the course of the meeting, the revolutionaries lay out the ideals that guide them.

> SSU 14, *Imperial China from the First Emperor to Kublai Khan*. The role of emperors; everyday life; the role of men and women and different generations.

Children pay their respects to a Chinese Emperor by bringing gifts. The ceremony is based on previous research. Different students play the role of Emperor in each new run of the ceremony. Simple percussion is integrated into the ceremonial chant which accompanies the Emperor's entrance.

> SSU 17, *Indigenous people of North America*. Settlements; cults, rituals and ceremonies.

American Indians conduct a marriage ceremony for two of their young people.

> SSU 18, *Black peoples of the Americas: 16 to early 20 centuries*. The material lives and working conditions of slaves; opposition to slavery; slave resistance and the revolts.

Teacher in role as William Wilberforce is hot-seated by a range of students in role. The teacher has written the role cards for plantation owners; slave trade shipowners; ships' crew members; fellow philanthropists; slaves; relatives of slaves left behind in Africa; free men; representatives of the Christian church; Lord Mansfield.

Specific content is not suggested in Key Stage 4, but it is reasonable to assume that students would be capable of the most sophisticated use of drama at this level, moving between techniques with confidence and ease.

Drama and music

The relationship between drama and music goes back to the dawn of time. The religious rituals of ancient tribes were a fusion of dance, vocal and instrumental sound, special costume, masks, body paint and drama. The relationship survives in much theatre, most dance and the music of film. Many educational productions incorporate music, and such occasions can provide an excellent context for musical composition and performance. There is a range of other more informal links which can be made in the day-to-day curriculum, especially in the primary school. HMI makes explicit references to drama in music, especially the opportunities for composing which exist in drama. In *The Teaching and Learning of Music*, they describe observations of good practice, many of which involve drama and movement (HMI, 1991). The National Curriculum underplays the relationships that exist between the two subjects in many schools and this is one area where teachers should follow their professional and creative judgement rather than be restricted by the documents.

At Key Stage (KS) 3, AT1, Programme of Study xi, requires students to: 'compose music in response to a wide range of stimuli, including the composition of music for special occasions'.

This could be interpreted as music for dramatic performance, both public work and the flexible and potentially more experimental activity within the curriculum.

In all such work, it is important that the needs of music do not become permanently subservient to those of drama, although generally it will be necessary for one or the other to have a leading role. The music specialist should be contacted early in the production planning process. This allows a productive relationship between the subjects to be negotiated, with time for the music composition to be properly integrated into the curriculum. Teachers of drama should be prepared to modify their performance ideas to accommodate the best use of the production for music students and take account of available resources. There will be times when the musical composition and performance will be undertaken by adults, but as far as possible, these responsibilities should be given to students.

Primary teachers are better able to achieve coherent curriculum contact between drama and music. Movement sequences and stories can be accompanied by appropriate music-making. Secondary drama and music teachers can co-operate to relate their subjects to common curriculum projects. Groups who devise movement sequences can create musical accompaniment to suit their requirements. This can either be taped or played live by another group within the class. Music to link scenes together in a polished class presentation, as described in Chapter 7, could be composed by that class and recorded. Alternatively, with two classes working in parallel, one group might learn and play live the music composed by the other, and vice versa. Many possibilities exist for exploiting this kind of activity. Goodwill, early planning and professional imagination can provide exciting contexts for music-making.

These possibilities are flagged within the music document. Attainment Target 1, Performing and Composing, has an example in 1d: 'create a musical pattern to match a movement pattern and teach it to another child', which exactly matches the curriculum exercise outlined above. Key Stage 1, AT1, Programme of Study (POS) ix: 'create, select and organise sounds in response to different stimuli' could be covered by allowing students to compose music in relation to an enactment of a folk tale –

> *What kind of music do we make when the giant wakes up?*
>
> *Can you work out some music for the rain and wind?*
>
> *We need a song that everyone can sing when the animals arrive.*

AT2, Listening and Appraising, 2b states:

> discuss how music composed for different celebrations and festivals creates appropriate moods.

This could be extended by the composition of appropriate accompaniment for rituals devised in drama, involving vocal music, percussion and instruments on which individuals are proficient. The use of electronic keyboards and computer programs can also be related to drama with the latter giving instant access to compositions through disk loading.

Also in this section is the example: 'discuss how sounds are used to describe the different animals in Saint-Saëns' *Carnival of the Animals.*' This discussion could be extended to develop movement sequences based on animal characteristics and musical imagery. At Key Stage 1, AT2, POS iv:

> listen and talk about a variety of live and recorded music exhibiting contrasts of style, including works by well known composers and performers as well as their own and others' compositions and improvisations.

Music could be used as a stimulus for drama. Just to consider one genre, carefully chosen extracts from Bartok's *The Miraculous Mandarin*, Stravinsky's *Rite of Spring* or Copland's *Fanfare for the Common Man* should engender a strong response. The ambiguity of music is one of its most intriguing features and the images groups experience through the music and create within the drama are often quite diverse.

Although film music generally differs in function from music in drama and theatre, a study of music in film and television drama might provide an interesting stimulus to composition in drama. For older students, Prokofiev's work in *Alexander Nevsky* or the score written for *Henry V* by William Walton would stand examination as a contrast to the way music is used in television dramas.

It is important that students doing drama have ready access to music-making equipment. In the secondary school this usually means building up an alternative range to that held in the music room. Correct storage is essential; items such as drum-skins and the heads of maracas are particularly vulnerable to damage.

Drama and art

As with music, curriculum co-operation between drama and art must not make the latter the junior partner. Related activities in the secondary school should be planned well in advance, allowing teachers to derive the maximum benefit for pupils and subject. Creative teaching, especially in the primary school, will throw up a variety of possibilities for drama/art-related work. The following suggestions derive directly from the art National Curriculum documents.

AT1, POS iii, Key Stage (KS)1: 'look and talk about examples of work of well known artists from a variety of periods and cultures' could be the starting point for story in drama. Having looked at a variety of pictures in art, students could choose one to bring alive, using the technique of inventing what happened in the periods before and after the instant shown in the painting. Alternatively, a completely new visual image might be presented as a stimulus for dramatic activity; follow-up discussion in art could feed off the sense of time, atmosphere, characterization and tension sensed in the drama.

AT1, POS viii, KS1: 'explore the shape, form and space in making images and artefacts' could encompass mask-making. Face painting could be used as an introduction to masks, and used in its own right in dramatic rituals and ceremony. Masks could be made in a variety of materials, experimenting with colour, texture and form (see Chapter 3). They could be viewed as artefacts in their own right before or after being used in drama.

Costumes that involve freehand painting direct on to material, stencilling, spray painting and appliqué can be designed and produced by students. Seams can be glued together to avoid machining processes, which may be too advanced for very young students. Decorative materials can be glued to the basic costume – sequins to catch light, for instance.

AT1, POS vii, KS3: 'explore and experiment with materials, images and ideas for three-dimensional work and realise their intentions', and the example given: 'use experimental materials. . . to design and make a range of body ornaments; neck-piece, bracelet, armlet, pendant', could link strongly with drama based on ancient cultures such as the Mayas and Incas, with further obvious links with music, geography and history. The costumes and properties for a school production could be designed and produced in art lessons, giving students responsibility for decisions about style, material, decoration, texture and colour. Larger three-dimensional pieces might be used as scenery and properties for production work – the design and execution of periaktoi, the tall revolving columns originally used in Greek theatre, which can be rotated to achieve scene changes; the painting of cardboard boxes used as background for a mime production; a mobile suspended in light above a dance performance.

AT1, POS v, KS3: 'use a wide range of media and techniques to realise their ideas, express feelings and communicate meaning', and the example given: 'design and print a poster. . . to advertise a school function' permits the production of play posters, handbills and programmes. It could also apply to photographs of dramatic form in mime, mask work, movement and productions, as drama provides challenging imagery for photographers and the products can help in promoting drama in school and community.

Work in this area might also encompass the production of a tape/slide programme which could be integrated into drama.

Primary students might construct large-scale objects to support their drama, using junk materials such as cardboard boxes together with paper and paint for decorating surfaces. Boats, cars, moon buggies and domestic or workplace environments are some examples. Such structures could be scaled up from small models created in the classroom.

The feelings and ideas experienced in creating something in art could be used as a stimulus in drama. Young students who complete collages on firework patterns could follow this up with firework movement sequences; or a group might improvise being in the world represented in the painting of one of their members. As with music, it is hoped that all the exciting work that took place between drama and art before the National Curriculum came into being will be maintained.

Drama and physical education (PE)

Dance forms one of the specified areas of study for PE, and is represented in all four Key Stages. As movement is an essential component of the drama vocabulary, it is important that teachers of drama and dance in secondary schools decide what will be discrete and what shared. There is considerable scope for co-operation, one example being the integration into drama of dances worked out in dance lessons, and vice versa. Dance and drama specialists must ensure that students are not confused by conflicting conventions and vocabularies.

Many schools see drama as part of a creative or expressive arts grouping, and teachers in such schools will have no problem developing fruitful links between the arts and between the arts and other areas of the curriculum. Material from non-arts lessons will quite naturally come to form the focus for artistic exploration and communication, resulting in a valuable model of coherence. Students come to see the arts as legitimate modes of expression for ideas that have originated in other disciplines.

Whilst dance and drama could each be said to have 'pure form' which excludes the other, imaginative and creative curriculum planning will reveal possible and necessary overlap. Specific mention is made of this in the Key Stage 2 Programmes of study:

> Pupils should: make dances with clear beginnings, middles and ends involving improvising, exploring, selecting and refining content, and sometimes incorporating work from other aspects of the curriculum, in particular music, art and drama. (NCC, 1992a)

There may be other opportunities to link the physical aspects of drama to PE, especially through physical work such as mime, certain circus skills and fights.

Drama and technology

At the time of writing, the Secretary of State is conducting a consultation exercise on revised orders for technology. Teachers had found it very difficult to implement the original orders and the new ones propose a halving of both attainment targets and statements of attainment (DFE, 1992). The following advice is given in the expectation that the revised orders will bear a strong similarity to the consultation document.

Drama's relationship with technology is most evident in the making of artefacts for use in drama lessons or productions, the design and manufacture of which would cover a large number of the programme of study elements in technology's two attainment targets, Designing and Making, and the supporting programmes of study: 'Business and Industrial Practices', 'Structures', 'Control Systems and Energy', 'Construction Materials and Components', and 'Food'. Design and making processes would involve defining the needs of the people who will use the product, production of a design brief and prototype, making the actual equipment and evaluation of its efficacy against previous intentions.

Examples of suitable pieces of equipment are: puppets; puppet booth; shadow puppet booth and articulated puppets; masks; props; a battery-operated doorbell/chime board for sound-effect use; a motorized flicker wheel for silent movie work; directional and dimmable lighting for control desks and panels; storage units for CDs, tapes, hand props or costumes; soundproofing of a booth or cupboard for sound recording; a warning light to show when such a space is in use; a display of text and photographs to promote drama or a specific production; rostra; stage set; a tester to check electrical continuity in leads and fuses; an electronic device, for use in mime and movement work, which produces sound signals of varying pitch, repeat rate, volume and rhythm; gobos; lighting stands and brackets.

The design and making processes should not be rushed, so drama teachers must identify a need well ahead of anticipated use of the equipment.

Examples of design-and-make tasks given in the consultation document include:

KS1: To design and make puppets with controlled moving parts based on observations of the movement of body joints.

This has obvious links with drama.

KS2: To design and make exit/entry points and defences for a settlement.

This example is set in the context of History Study Unit 1 ('Invaders and Settlers'). The work could be enhanced and extended by the creation through drama of the settlement and its inhabitants, including representations of the design solutions.

KS3: To design and make a food product. . . (for pupils on a hill-walking expedition).

This could be reinterpreted in the context of the suitability of refreshment for an audience of a public performance.

Such work could be extended into the major organizational aspects of school productions which would have real outcomes for evaluation.

Elements of the supporting programme of study, 'Business and Industrial Practices' would be met in planning and executing the publicity, tickets and programmes, refreshment, front-of-house displays and other arrangements for a performance. If properties, costumes and set were included, further areas of the attainment targets could be met. Proper co-operation should avoid the feeling that the technology department is simply the servant of drama when it comes to the school play. All can now see how such co-operation can serve the needs of technology. Once again, teachers of drama need to involve the technology teacher at the planning stage.

> KS4: To design and make a folding structure . . . capable of housing two . . . slide projectors and a tape recorder.

This could be reinterpreted in relation to a need to store or support projection or sound equipment in a drama space, or the construction of folding or nesting rostra.

The document refers a number of times to students' awareness of the values of consumers and how these are reflected in the products they buy. Improvisation could be used here to embed these topics in a simulated human context, looking at such issues as life-style, spending power, peer-group pressure and psychological factors of consumer choice and preference.

The greater flexibility of the primary school again makes it much easier to bring drama and technology together. Beside the actual use in drama of artefacts produced in technology, primary-age students would take readily to exploring modelled environments or objects. The model castle produced in the classroom might be represented in the hall by the use of rostra, PE equipment, cardboard boxes, tubes from the centre of carpet rolls and other available material. Having posited what kind of people live in the castle, students could act out aspects of their lives in the built environment.

Design processes will include considerations of fitness for purpose. Drama might allow students to explore this concept in human contexts that help them understand the factors which influenced an object's purpose, shape and material of manufacture:

> What was life like with candles or oil lamps for illumination?
> What kind of family used that old valve radio?
> What was childhood like for the children who bowled this iron hoop?
> Which people might have used this mortar and pestle, and what did they make with it?

In each case, the scenes developed around these objects could be contrasted with scenes which feature their modern equivalents – electric light, personal stereo, Nintendo Game Boy, bottle of aspirin tablets.

The document states: 'The area of values was considered to be essential as a context for design and technology activity' (ibid., p.50). This gives scope for exploration of ethical aspects of technological development, especially environmental impact.

Drama and modern foreign languages

Role play, in the restricted sense described in Chapter 3, is now used extensively in foreign-language lessons. Language is a living form and the use of drama techniques allows it to be exercised in situations which effectively mirror real life. Many students are reluctant to speak a foreign language in situations where error or lack of knowledge may cause embarrassment, and the great strength of using drama is its ability to give a situation the dynamic interpersonal momentum that requires participants to respond. In doing this, students tend to forget the gaps in their knowledge and put to best use the language skills they currently possess. Taking part in an improvisation where you are trying to explain to a foreign garage mechanic the nature of the knocking in your car engine should, with all the body language possibilities, carry you through any feelings of language incompetence.

The subject has four attainment targets. Drama would be of particular use in AT1, Listening and AT2, Speaking, although exercises such as writing in role following a drama activity – questioning the bill received from the garage, for instance – could help in AT4, Writing. Role play and improvised drama are suggested as necessary techniques in the Non-Statutory Guidance (NCC, 1992b, pp. E7, H8). The programmes of study suggest areas of learning in the language being studied. They include:

> communicating in the target language, understanding and responding, developing cultural awareness and developing the ability to work with others.

Suggested areas of experience are:

> everyday activities, personal and social life, the world around us, the world of education, training and work, the world of communications, the international world and the world of imagination and creativity.

Drama has a natural place in all these areas. The following examples will, I hope, demonstrate how the use of drama creates situations where the struggle to communicate overrides feelings of inadequacy.

139

Students who have sound knowledge of a language may go straight into improvisations in an effort to practise that which they already know. Those who are less skilled may need to carry out a thorough review of the situation's language demands before entering into it. Discussion and practice of vocabulary that may be of use in the situation to be dramatized can be of great help. Teachers should severely restrict or ban the use of English within improvisation lest students choose the easy way out. Debriefing, which addresses the outcome of the drama, the foreign language use and further needs, should follow the improvisation.

There are obvious benefits from 'teacher in role' approaches which allow the teacher to sustain the momentum of the work and to match language use to the ability of the students. The teacher could be hot-seated: as the following characters, for example:

- a foreign national who speaks no English and has caught the wrong train at Gatwick and arrived, confused, at the school. She needs advice on where she is, and how she might get to her correct destination. Maps of both countries are to hand;
- a foreign national puzzled by some aspect of British culture and seeking guidance;
- a foreign researcher who speaks no English, wanting information on how much the British students know about her country.

Improvisations in pairs gives each student maximum opportunity to use the foreign language. Possible situations might include:

A German and a Spanish student meet on holiday in France. Neither speaks the other's language, but both speak some French, so, in that language, they talk about the camp site they are in.

A foreign customs official who speaks no English opens the suitcase of a British visitor and discovers it to be full of illegal goods. An explanation is required.

Group work should normally follow a thorough grounding in drama approaches which allow foreign-language use in safe structures. Group situations should encourage improvisation within the chosen language rather than devising 'British abroad' scenarios. It is essential that the improvisation contain opportunities for action to avoid the drama being overly reliant on the constant use of the language. Here are some examples:

Three workers have almost finished double-glazing a house. The owner returns to tell them the work should have been done on the next-door property.

Four motorists arrive at the same parking space at the same time and each declares reasons why she should be allowed to park there.

Three customers approach the owner of a launderette to complain that their clothes have been shredded by the washing machine and then burned by the tumble-drier.

Drama could assist in the teaching of specific statements of attainment. The following are examples only:

AT1, 3a: understand and respond to short instructions, messages and dialogues made up of familiar language in sentences.

Here students might carry out a particular mime, changing the nature of their actions in response to statements made by a partner –

You drop two eggs and step in them.

The spoon is stuck in the mixture.

The flour goes all over your clothes.

AT2, 4a: initiate and respond in conversation or role play on familiar topics using appropriate forms of personal address.

Person A is a policeman or woman, person B a British person on a foreign holiday who has lost a camera with some rather embarrassing photos in it.

Person A, a foreign customs officer, is explaining to person B what quantity of duty-free goods he may take through customs.

Each of these situations would allow students to augment their foreign-language use with mime. Class discussion should precede the improvisation to identify words – commonly nouns, adjectives, verbs and adverbs – and phrases which may be of use in the drama. These should be displayed in such a way that participants can glance at them for guidance. If the main reason for using the drama is to encourage students to communicate through the language, they should not be overly conscious of accuracy. This can be dealt with in follow-up work if required.

Drama and religious education

The Education Reform Act 1988 requires schools to provide religious education for all registered students, including those in Years 12 and

13. Religious education is included in the basic curriculum by law but the NCC was not charged with producing a curriculum document as the subject was to be taught within locally agreed syllabuses. Each local education authority has therefore developed its own syllabus or agreed to adopt one developed by another LEA. My ideas for links between drama and RE are based on an examination of the agreed syllabus produced by Devon County Council (1992). The document maintains that religious education should assist students to: 'reflect on those aspects of human experience which give rise to fundamental questions about life' (ibid., p.10). It further maintains that RE should provide students with opportunities to think about moral and ethical issues and to make and evaluate choices related to them.

Drama's ability to set these aspects of the subject within a believable human context should make its approaches central to the teaching of RE, where values and attitudes are best examined in relation to the actuality of an everyday setting. Forum theatre is particularly useful in exploring situations that involve moral choice, as variables can be modified in an examination of cause and effect. In a situation where a student finds out that a friend is stealing from the local shop, the improvisation could be run several times, changing such factors as the attitudes of all parties, the value of the goods stolen and the background and family circumstances of the thief. Alternatively, the teacher might work a class in pairs, all basically dealing with the same situation, but with some changed variables in each group.

In an attempt to explore the potential conflict between religious and certain secular values, the role cards featuring Elizabeth and David Price contained in Chapter 5 (see pp.68–9) might be adapted for use in an RE class with Year 10 or 11 students. Student pairs would be assigned to one of four sub-groups, and each group would be given role cards with certain variables changed:

The improvisations can be run to their conclusions and the students asked to respond as self, or they can be stopped as you see the first pair finishing – see guidance on end-of-improvisation signalling in Chapter 3 (see p.20) – and the characters questioned in role. If the latter approach is used, the teacher would probably not want to question each pair, but would choose at least one pair to represent each sub-group.

Similar concepts could be explored in different age-groups if the circumstances were modified. With Year 6 students, the issue might be the kinds of video the child watches at friends' houses or the preference of the son to mix with friends who are not of the faith and do not share his values.

Group 1 – a Muslim household. The parent has become increasingly frustrated by the behaviour of the son and this incident is the last straw. Strict instructions about mixing with non-Muslim friends and the avoidance of alcohol appear to have been ignored.

Group 2 – a Jewish household, but not a strict one. The parent has been thinking recently about her own, rather rebellious, teenage years, comparing them with those of the son in an attempt to decide what sort of behaviour to expect in a modern Jewish family. She is nevertheless disturbed by the son's behaviour.

Group 3 – a devout Christian household. The son, a believer, feels that, compared with friends, he is overly restricted by the parent's 'rules'. He also detects a certain hypocrisy, given there is no father in the home.

Group 4 – the mother is a lapsed Catholic, the son a practising Catholic. He welcomes the open discussion about what is/is not permissible and respects his mother's attempts to introduce him to adulthood progressively although he detects elements of hypocrisy in her argument.

Drama could be used to investigate such concepts as wealth and poverty, hunger and plenty, autonomy and authority, rights and responsibilities, honesty and integrity, conflict, justice, dignity and compassion. Many of the structures employed as examples for drama use in other subjects would be appropriate in RE.

Religions usually embody some sense of mystery and forms of ritual. These areas could be explored through drama, with students comparing ritual form and content from different cultures, subsequently developing their own when the elements of ritual and ceremony – symbolism, sacred places, religious artefacts, for instance – have been identified.

Drama and special educational needs

The National Curriculum Council defines special needs students as falling into four groups. They are:

1 Pupils with exceptionally severe learning difficulties;
2 Pupils with other learning difficulties;
3 Pupils with physical or sensory impairment;
4 Exceptionally able pupils.

(NCC, 1993b)

Drama can make a significant contribution to the education of students in the above categories. For those with learning difficulties, drama provides an expressive form which couples thought to action, giving immediate results. Drama can be liberating in that it employs communication forms other than writing. Perhaps drama's most obvious use here is to provide structured opportunities for language development, but it can also make significant contributions to physical and emotional development.

Drama activity should be based on clear and easily appreciated ideas. Teachers may need to give particular consideration to creating a safe environment and supportive atmosphere, where behavioural limits are clearly understood by all concerned. Whilst it is essential that the students become engaged with the drama and respond with enthusiasm, it is important that they are 'wound down' before the session ends. The use of other adults as helpers can facilitate drama work. It is advisable to consult doctors, physiotherapists and other relevant professionals when devising programmes of activity. The following examples are illustrative of approaches which might be used in working with special needs students.

Students with exceptionally severe learning difficulties

Physical environments can be built using the large, soft, three-dimensional shapes often found in special schools. Structures can be personalized by the addition of signs, cloths and paintings, and signs can be word- or symbol-based. Students might make journeys through these structures, meeting people who role-play characters who might be found in such locations. Interaction – vocal or otherwise – would be appropriate to the abilities of the students. The drama experience might involve other sensory experiences to do with music, mirrors, projected images and tactile experience. Students may be presented with choices – for example, of routes, sounds, images, characters to meet. Building such a structure may be time consuming, but careful planning would enable it to be used by the maximum number of students.

Pupils with other learning difficulties

The National Curriculum Council document states that this category may include students with 'specific learning difficulties where language development (both spoken and written) proves problematic' and who have 'emotional and behavioural difficulties' (ibid). Drama can aid language development, as its 'as if' situations demand responses related to specific contexts. These contexts can be arranged in order to practise particular oral skills, for instance, buying things in shops or visiting the library, which might then be employed in a real situation. Drama's ability to animate knowledge gained elsewhere in the curriculum can be exploited, for example, dramatizing a favourite story; dramas based around a visit to the zoo, castle or beach.

Drama can provide contexts in which students with emotional and behavioural difficulties can come to terms with situations with which they find difficulty in coping. Drama can help in the development of social skills. Such work borders on drama therapy, and teachers who regularly employ these approaches should seek further guidance from a qualified drama therapist.

Pupils with physical or sensory impairment

The drama experience should be tailored to individual need. Once again, drama's main contribution lies in its ability to create situations which parallel those of real life, giving the teacher opportunities to target particular experiences for students. Physically disabled students could make drama within a safe but challenging environment; hearing impaired students might explore a situation which will make particular demands on them; visually impaired students might dramatize a particularly physical story in the knowledge that the space is surrounded by soft block screening.

Exceptionally able pupils

'It is a teacher's duty to ensure that progress through the National Curriculum for these pupils is in line with their abilities' (ibid.).

Teachers will meet students who show an exceptional ability in drama. Such students seem to have an innate sense of how different aspects of the medium work, and they quickly demonstrate impressive control of their bodies and voices. Their creative sophistication and enthusiasm often lifts the work of other students in the group and the flexible nature of drama often provides excellent opportunities for them to interpret ideas at their own very high level. At appropriate ages, teachers should encourage these very able students to attend drama clubs, join youth theatres, experience residential courses and see good theatre. These are the rights of all students of course, but it is particularly important that those who have marked aptitudes in drama are allowed and encouraged to develop them.

Chapter 9

DRAMA AND THE
CROSS-CURRICULAR PROJECT

> The good news for teachers is that the arrival of the National Curriculum
> will be an impetus towards creating a coherent whole. The bad news is that
> the NCC is not yet ready with practical advice about how to achieve this
> splendid goal. (Hargreaves, 1990, p.18)

The National Curriculum was conceived as ten separate subjects.
Subject working groups submitted their reports to the Minister, who
often made significant changes to the recommended subject structure
and content before their introduction in schools. David Hargreaves
regrets that little time was devoted to making the separate subjects
cohere:

> One of the best ideas that HMI contributed to the debate was the principle
> that the curriculum should be 'broad, balanced and coherent'. The DES
> adopted the notion of broad and balanced but somehow and for unknown
> reasons the concept of coherence was quietly dropped. Yet to me it is one of
> the most important principles. (ibid.)

The NCC has attempted to introduce some binding mortar to the
individual subject blocks. There are cross-curricular dimensions (such
as personal and social education), cross-curricular skills (oracy,
numeracy, literacy, as well as problem-solving and study skills), and
cross-curricular themes (careers, health education, environmental
education, citizenship and economic and industrial understanding).
The introduction of cross-curricular themes and dimensions could be
seen to stem from the discontinuation of previously discrete curriculum
areas such as TVEI and personal and social education. The NCC seems
to have totalled the content of the ten subject areas, recognized some
gaps, and attempted to plug them with cross-curricular requirements.
Most judge them to be poor substitutes for the whole-curriculum planning required to achieve the coherence which Hargreaves, amongst
many others, calls for:

> From the point of view of the DES, this was a means of solving the quart
> into a pint pot problem. The subjects excluded from the National
> Curriculum, we were blithely informed, should be taught as themes
> through foundation subjects. (ibid.)

The NCC has published guidance which suggests that they wish primary teachers to view the curriculum and their approach to teaching it in a more flexible manner than the separate subject ring-binders would suggest. The introduction to 'Curriculum Guidance 1' states:

> The description of the National Curriculum in terms of foundation subjects is not a description of how the school day should be organised or the curriculum delivered. (NCC, 1989c, p.1)

Elsewhere in its documentation, the NCC acknowledges the central place of 'cross-curricular elements' of a more general nature. It terms them: the 'ingredients which tie together the broad education of the individual and augment what comes from the basic curriculum' (NCC, 1990b, p.2).

Examples given include how history might explore conflicting motives, technology the political, social and moral implications of decision-making and how science may cast light on ways in which scientific ideas are affected by the social, moral and spiritual context in which they develop (ibid.).

The value of cross-curricular learning

To many teachers, especially those in the primary sector, the notion that students should not experience a 'whole curriculum' is abhorrent. Jon Nixon feels that the very use of the term by the NCC suggests they see the curriculum they have created as anything but whole:

> The notion of 'the whole curriculum' is perhaps, therfore, a necessary rhetorical device only when the very idea of curriculum coherence is at risk. (Nixon, 1991, p.187)

Nixon argues that for true coherence to be achieved, teachers must re-establish their pre-eminent role as professional decision-takers and regain the curriculum initiative:

> [the curriculum must be seen as] a process that must be constantly renewed by teachers critically engaging with their own practice and relating that practice, through collegial discussion and self-reflection, to their own espoused values. (ibid., p.191)

The pursuit of a whole curriculum can be furthered by the introduction of well-planned cross-curricular learning. Such activity can only be worth contemplating if it enhances the educational experience of students, and when it functions effectively, the whole is greater than the sum of the parts. The chief benefit results from the way knowledge can become integrated, providing a coherent understanding of a topic area which has been viewed from different subject standpoints. Such teaching often gives priority to students' active role in their own learning. It also encourages teacher co-operation, invention of new structures and the very stuff of professional decision-making which many believe to have been curtailed by the introduction of the National Curriculum.

The primary school

In primary schools, integrated learning is commonplace and, despite expressing the curriculum in terms of ten subject areas, the NCC expects this to continue: 'For young children it is usually inappropriate to view the curriculum – from the point of view of the learner – as separate subjects' (NCC, 1989c, p.20).

Because one teacher may cover the majority of the teaching in a class, there is far greater opportunity for knowledge to be co-ordinated and for the timetable to be less rigidly operated. This is not to say that the primary teacher can ignore the complex demands of the new curriculum, simply that she has more opportunity to relate areas of subject content within a more flexible organization and environment.

Figures 9.1 and 9.2 show a model of topic planning and how to plan a topic in relation to the whole curriculum (Wiltshire County Council, 1989, pp.4 and 5).

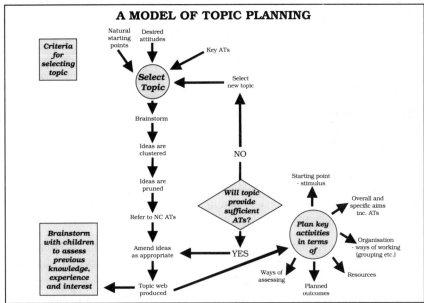

Figure 9.1 A model of topic planning

Figure 9.1 shows how primary teachers can absorb attainment target requirements into a process which gives them professional control of the National Curriculum.

Because of its inclusion in the English statutory requirements, drama should be embedded in all topics planned in relation to the whole curriculum. Drama approaches provide ways into many aspects of the topic and are a valuable medium for the communication of project outcomes.

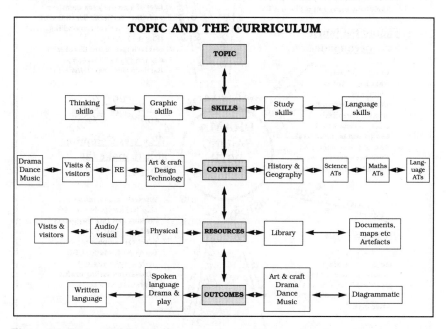

Figure 9.2 Topic and the curriculum

A topic web model with drama at the centre of work on Columbus in a primary school is shown in Figure 9.3. This was devised by Joe Winston, a lecturer in education at Warwick University. It shows how teachers may have to adapt the needs of the National Curriculum to achieve coherence.

The secondary school

In secondary schools, the organizational form of cross-curricular work can range from discrete subject area teaching which addresses a common theme, to sophisticated models of team teaching which require major revisions of class groupings and teaching spaces. In practice, sustained cross-curricular work is usually of limited scope.

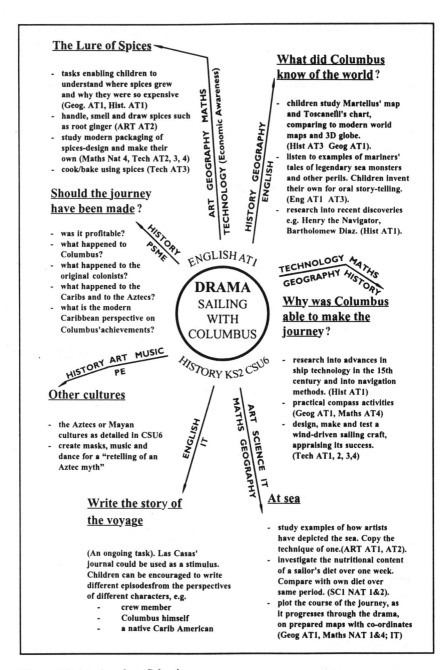

Figure 9.3 A topic web on Columbus

Curriculum organization and examination requirements tend to stifle co-operation, and the demands of a subject-specific National Curriculum have left little time for teachers to plan outside their specialisms.

This is articulated by Lyn Dent, a Community Education Tutor at Ivybridge Community College in Devon:

> I think everyone is so tied up with getting the National Curriculum taught that they have no time to think about education in a wider way anymore. And that is very, very sad. (Croall, 1992, p.75)

Normally, in secondary schools, teachers do not concern themselves with what is being taught in other areas, but a cross-curricular approach demands they see their teaching in relation to the students' general educational experience. We expect students to make sense of what we teach in relation to everything else they know and it therefore seems bizarre not to take account of the generality of the curriculum when we serve up our subject's offering.

> Traditionally the curriculum has lacked coherence at the level of the teachers. If the curriculum could be described as a secret garden, then in secondary schools subject specialists tended their own secret garden and hid the content from colleagues teaching different subjects. More importantly, the secondary curriculum lacked coherence for pupils. To them it was indeed what HMI rightly condemned: just a collection of subjects. (Hargreaves, 1990, p.18)

To make liaison, planning, teaching and evaluation manageable, secondary cross-curricular work is often limited to co-operation between small numbers of teachers and subjects. The bilateral contacts between drama and other subjects described in Chapter 8 come into this category.

Worthwhile cross-subject teaching requires imagination, hard graft, flexibility – not least from senior management and timetablers – and a sense of humour! It is not for the faint-hearted, but considerable satisfactions are to be gained for those who do take part. If the project is to retain its integrity, staff need to meet regularly to review progress and to adapt their planning to the organic change which inevitably occurs: 'The problem is that such enormous cross-curricular provision needs to be co-ordinated within itself by teachers' (ibid.).

The process of more complex schemes can be expedited by a co-ordinator who should, if possible, be given some timetable relief in the planning and execution phases of the project. It is best to restrict the participating subjects to those where teachers have shown enthusiasm to be involved. This may make a less than balanced scheme, but is more likely to ensure success and preserve professional relationships. Having witnessed a successful first attempt, sceptics may join an interdisciplinary venture more willingly the second time round.

The benefits of cross-curricular teaching were evident in the biggest series of co-ordinated cross-curricular projects ever undertaken in Britain. The Calouste Gulbenkian Foundation funded 'Dig Where You Stand', a scheme which required the 60 participating schools to make use of primary source material in researching aspects of their communities and to reflect their findings to the community in some form of presentation. Philip Waring, Head of Expressive Arts at Diss High School, highlights the opportunities for staff co-operation:

> If you want to bring staff together who would not normally work together, this is actually a very good way of doing it. You've got to have a way in, and this was it. An inter-disciplinary approach like this should be part of every school's experience. In curriculum terms, the number of hours spent was tiny. But the effect on the kids was out of all proportion. (Croall, 1992, p.50)

The 'Dig Where You Stand' projects had in common a final presentation. The presentational forms included dance productions, art and documentary exhibitions and slide shows, but the one most used was drama.

The place of drama

It is clearly not necessary or desirable for all cross-curricular projects to end in performance. The need is for students to 'broadcast' the outcomes of such work and this can take place through exhibitions of art and written work, displays of artefacts, published material and student presentations. This is done to reveal, for general appreciation, the material covered during the project, but also to provide a summative expression of what students and teachers consider the more interesting aspects of learning. The selecting, ordering and communicating of the fruits of the work are important final stages in most cross-curricular projects.

Where drama is used as a focus for a project, its eclectic nature and flexible structures allow the drawing together of material covered in disparate areas of the curriculum. Long-term preparation of a drama presentation provides a filter through which students sift relevant topic material, organizing their selection through rehearsal for performance. Performances can be augmented by exhibitions, displays and publications which cover topic material relevant to, but not directly covered by, the performance.

Drama can provide an ideal focus and catalyst for appropriate interdisciplinary work. Both in the process – where improvisation gives form to lives being studied – and as a major means of communicating outcomes, it can provide the contexts in which subject knowledge is applied. Its ability to bring material alive is recognized by HMI:

> Whilst drama deals with people and the ways in which they develop through time, it always happens in the present. Events are enacted or unfold before our eyes, so it is a powerful way of bringing alive knowledge and experience which might otherwise be inert. (HMI, 1989, p.1)

Suggestions for using drama as an exploratory medium are dealt with in Chapters 2 and 4, and drama as performance in a cross-curricular context is exemplified in Chapter 10. Here I will give a skeletal example of how drama might be threaded through a cross-curricular study. The work outlined would be suitable for top junior or lower secondary students.

Victorian climbing boys

The areas listed below would be studied during the project period which would last six weeks in all. The final shaping and performance of the play which forms a central focus for all of the work would extend for a further two weeks. The sequence of teaching in each subject would be co-ordinated to maximize the relationship between areas of learning. In the secondary school, thorough planning would be required to ensure that participating teachers were aware of the overall goals and how their topic content related to that in other subjects. If the work was confined to one primary class, the teacher would have total control of the project. If more than one class is to be involved, considerable discussion and liaison time would be needed.

- Social conditions of the time (history);
- Social reformers (history);
- Political context (history);
- Examination of first-hand testimony and evidence (English/history) (e.g. Carpenter, 1972);
- Maps of the period (geography);
- Public health (science);
- Occupational disease (science);
- Housing (geography/technology/maths);
- Education (history);
- Coal-burning fires (technology/science);
- The nature of tar and soot (science);
- Layout of chimneys (maths);
- The moral tone of early-nineteenth-century society (RE);

- Child labour and the church (RE);
- The economics of the nineteenth century (history);
- Popular and folk songs, hymns and patriotic music of the period (music);
- *The Water Babies* (English);
- Illustrative art (art);
- Domestic heating today (technology);
- Acid rain and other pollutants (science);
- Modern chimney-sweeping (technology);
- Literature of the period – factual (Mayhew, 1950) and fictional (Dickens) (English);
- Infant mortality/life-span and other statistical information (maths);
- Child labour today (geography/RE).

These subject topics are easily related to subject attainment targets. Teachers need to acquire effective resource material, some of which may be specially created, and staff must meet regularly to check the project's efficacy. The presence of a co-ordinator provides a focus for participating staff. The co-ordinator should have a day-to-day awareness of events and outcomes, guiding changes of approach or timetabling to take advantage of serendipity and initiating programme changes which result from the organic nature of the work.

Drama lessons would occur throughout the life of the project, their prime purpose being to examine the human implications of knowledge gained elsewhere. A maths lesson which considers the layout of houses and chimneys could be followed by a drama session dealing with the difficulties of entering and working in such spaces. Knowledge gained in lessons on public health in science and social conditions in history might be used in developing family groupings in drama. At some point towards the middle of the project period, drama time would be taken up with developing the performance. By this time the students should be empowered by their knowledge of the topic and be confident in finding any additional information required. As the form of the performance develops, subject area teaching can be adapted to take account of knowledge required for the drama. In the secondary school, subject teachers should be drawn into the production process. This is easily achieved if the production has the unit format described in Chapter 7 where individual units are under the organization of a different teacher. Each unit would focus on a different topic area, with the units linked to provide a coherent production. The following is an example of a scenario for a production which might result from the cross-curricular project on climbing boys:

1   **Living conditions** – a poor family contemplates its lot. Father suggests that son Samuel become a chimney-boy. Mother, protective, objects. Boy says he will go as he can see how even the small amount he will earn will benefit the family.

2   **The work of chimney boys** – Father takes boy to an employer. Tries to lay down conditions for son's employment, but boss is a hard man. Father leaves, Samuel meets other boys. They tell him what to expect. Some rag him. Put to his first chimney – cut to mother and father talking as Samuel works.

3   **Medical convention** – scientists explain to assembled doctors the constituents of soot and related materials. Doctor explains the effects of chimney-boys' work on their health. Social reformer attempts to harness findings to her cause, but is ejected from the hall.

4   **Doctor's surgery** – Mother seeks help with the first serious signs of illness in Samuel. Doctor is of the 'old school' and feels Mother is worrying unduly. Mother accuses him of complacency. Samuel embarrassed as doctor throws fees back to Mother and asks her to leave.

5   **A group of social reformers organize and address a meeting** – employers, politicians and parents are present. A range of opinion is voiced. The reformer ejected from the medical convention asks parents of chimney-boys to volunteer them to provide evidence on working conditions.

6   **Samuel talks to the reformer** – flashbacks to his work as Samuel speaks – these are stylized, and do not include Samuel in person, although he may be addressed by others.

7   **Stylized collage of events leading up to the abolition of chimney-boys' jobs** – collage includes narration; newspaper extracts/headlines; snatches of parliamentary and other speeches; extracts from pertinent conversations; aspects of Samuel's life over time as he becomes ill.

8   **The celebration of the abolition of chimney-boys' jobs** – social reformers and sympathetic MPs address meeting which breaks up into a party. Speeches put abolition into general political/medical/social/educational context.

9   **Samuel's death** – the street party freezes and remains lit. A bell tolls. A cleric speaks the final words of the funeral service. Samuel's family mourn. A spotlit speaker rails against the conditions endured by children in factories and mills.

This outline is not comprehensive and may, through its brevity, seem melodramatic. My intention is to indicate how a cross-curricular project with educational and artistic integrity might work in a secondary school.

To make meaning of the material in a dramatic context, pupils and teachers would go through the following processes:

Researching

Identifying which aspects of the material covered within the project might be suitable for dramatization. If there is an overall framework for the play's content at the outset, it should be applied at this stage to provide a filter for selection.

Responding imaginatively

Investigating through discussion and writing the selected material's dramatic potential. Students may need to practise the backtracking approach outlined in Chapter 5. This stage involves individual and small group work in arriving at possible scenarios to be explored in improvisations.

Exploring

In this phase, students explore through practical work the potential identified in the preceding phase. In the production outlined above this exploration would mostly have taken the form of improvisation and reflective discussion. Students should have a firm grasp of the principles of improvisation set out in Chapter 3, especially the information which participants need to know before entering the action. When a scenario has been worked on, it should be 'put on the shelf' while others are attempted. Where the play's structure is developed in parallel with the exploration of material, students should be helped to see narrative and skill links between isolated unit scenarios as the work progresses. Material covered should be recorded for future reference through note-taking, sound or video recording and scripting. The latter can range from jotting down phrases which seem of particular use or merit, to scripting a scene from a transcript of a recording. See Chapter 6 for guidance.

Selecting

Once a store of material is acquired, students need to select aspects of it to create a performance piece. If the process already covered has not begun to suggest an overall scenario for the play, the collage of scenes will need to be examined to see where the main focus falls. A useful way of moving forward is to list all the material, plus the ideas which have emerged in the final discussions. Ask individuals or small groups to devise their own plot, preferably represented in diagrammatic form. Diagrams help as they physicalize and give shape to story, often suggesting scene divisions, character relationships and staging ideas through their very form. Discussion of these plot-lines can be a starting point for deciding the overall scenario. Be prepared to see this as a 'holding form' only, and allow the structure to develop organically as the following processes continue.

Ordering

An extension of selecting. Students experiment with restructuring elements of the play and its overall form. This process continues as the production is shaped.

Shaping

The polishing and final arranging of the material. In the early stages, changes may be made to the material and its positioning within the play. Scenes may be deleted, shortened, lengthened and added. Small changes may continue to be made right up to the performance.

Presenting

More than mere performance, for the performance may be accompanied by exhibitions, total theatre environments, complex programmes, refreshments to match and all the other ideas raised as useful adjuncts to dramatic work described elsewhere in this book. The presentation should be seen as the logical culmination of a process in which the students have moved from a state of relative or even complete ignorance of the area being studied to one where they handle the material with confidence, familiarity and skill. To witness and aid that process is one of the deepest satisfactions a teacher can experience. It is the teacher's task to put in place the complex and highly sophisticated frameworks required for the successful completion of such work.

Chapter 10

A CASE STUDY

I teach in the School of Education at Exeter University, and each year, students specializing in English and drama take part in co-operative projects with South-West schools. The projects I am about to describe were carried out in Exwick Middle School, Exeter. They were run by four teachers, fourteen university students and me, but I wish to stress that they could have been attempted, albeit in a modified way, without student teacher help. I therefore feel that they stand as appropriate models for teachers who contemplate something similar, as their structures and methodologies could be applied to content other than that used at Exwick, namely the history of school and community. I hope their chief use will be to show how drama can be a focus for sophisticated cross-curricular work.

The school and community

Exwick lies just north-west of Exeter, separated from the city by the River Exe. It is one of a number of small villages which, until recently, were geographically, socially and culturally distinct, but with the expansion of both city and villages, many now see Exwick as part of Exeter. The presence of the river was to be a constant theme in our work. Until the relatively recent completion of a flood-relief scheme, the lower parts of the community, including the old school, were repeatedly flooded, as an extract from the school log-book shows:

> *February 15, 1900* A continuous heavy fall of rain on the top of the previous snowfall caused a flood, which surrounded the school premises & filled the space under the floor. The water was just entering the inner door when it commenced to recede.

Exwick has expanded fortyfold in the last thirty years and the hillsides that overlook the river plain are covered in modern housing developments. Many old buildings remain, embedded in this enlarged community.

The students were able to identify a number of former farms, their landless farmhouses now mostly converted to suit late-twentieth-century urban living. We found one farm where the retired farmer, his holding reduced to a garden due to housing development, sat with his

Figure 10.1 Exwick in the floods

Figure 10.2 Housing estates have enlarged Exwick

dog and talked to us in the old barn. The village also has a mill, Priory Mill, originally built by monks in the thirteenth century and working as an animal feedstuffs concern until quite recently. The course of the mill leat can be traced for most of its route through the village, although new housing has blocked parts of it.

Figure 10.3 An old Exwick farm amid the new houses

The original school was built in 1890. A new school was built above the floodplain in 1971, the old school becoming a community centre, a function it still performs (Figures 10.5 and 10.6). The village hall and church are nearby, and the old school rubs shoulders with a tollhouse, built to house those who collected the dues for crossing the Exe using the 'new' bridge. Until that time, people forded the river in summer or made long treks up- or down-stream to cross by existing bridges.

Theatre and community

The parents of the students involved were mostly newcomers to the village and they had little knowledge of its history. One of our prime aims was to create opportunities for the students to discover and understand aspects of Exwick's past, and to articulate that to the community. We wanted to use the performances as a focus to celebrate and broadcast a shared culture. Ann Jellicoe, who has created

160

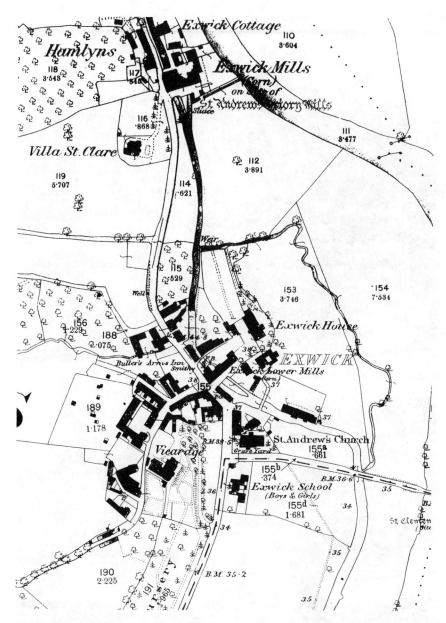

Figure 10.4 Ordnance map of Exwick, 1890

community plays in many West Country towns, recognizes the importance of this function:

> Communities need community events to continually refresh them. Community drama can be a celebration of community; discovering the nature of a community; articulating it *to* that community. (Jellicoe, 1987, p.46)

Figure 10.5 Exwick's old school

Figure 10.6 Exwick's new school

Benedict Nightingale, in the *New Statesman* of 9 October 1985, noted theatre's ability to work within a community to heighten people's awareness of where they live:

> Isn't it good that a community should learn more, more about the past that has shaped its present, the roots that have determined its identity? Isn't it good that it should deepen its understanding of itself; entertain itself?

The idea of using the surrounding community as a resource for learning is not new, and most schools conduct local studies. As I pointed out in Chapter 9, the 'Dig Where You Stand' projects were of this kind and many used drama as a focus for the work. HMI recognizes drama's aptness for this role:

> Material [for drama lessons] should draw upon local heritage and cultures, so that pupils can better understand both how their own community came to be and how it might develop. (HMI, 1989, p.12)

Exwick lacks many of the facilities which such a large concentration of housing would normally possess. It has very few shops, a small village hall and no natural focus for the community other than the school and the church. The school's curriculum work on local history and the plays that resulted were therefore particularly significant within this settlement.

The project format

The university students were split into two groups of seven. One group worked with two teachers and sixty students from Year 6 to produce a live performance dealing with Exwick in late Victorian times. The other group helped two teachers and thirty students from Year 7 develop a radio play based on happenings in Exwick around the time of the Second World War. During the course of the projects we benefited from the enthusiastic professionalism of the staff and the unflagging optimism and support of the headteacher, Ken Turner.

The Year 6 live project – 'When I Was a Boy'

The students followed the classic format laid out in Chapter 9 on pages 153–7. The two class teachers, Gill Palmer and Gary Read, covered a variety of material to do with the period under study, relating the topic to most of the foundation subjects. The aim of the history work was to set the local study, which was to be the focus of the project and the drama, within an effective understanding of national and world events. General curriculum work on the topic was under way for some

Figure 10.7 Research in the community

weeks before the notion of the play was introduced. The teachers used conventional curriculum approaches and materials to give the students a firm understanding of turn-of-the-century Britain, and in this context the students researched the history of their community.

Older people who had lived all their life in Exwick were invited to talk. Harold Ackland, a local amateur historian, was particularly useful, giving unstintingly of his time in showing artefacts and documents from the village's past. He also had a fund of stories about former residents and events. The usual resources – books, videos, slides, maps, documents from the County Record Office, local museum collections and field visits – were available, and teachers made good use of material which was brought in from families whose forebears had lived in the area since Victorian times. The students gained an understanding of the nature of Exwick life and the place of the school in the community through time.

Developing the drama

Once the curriculum work had been established for one month, the notion of the play was introduced. The children in both projects went through the same introductory process. This involved inferring story from the intriguingly sparse descriptions of events contained in the school's log-books. I read all the log-book entries and photocopied those which appeared to have most dramatic potential. The selection was presented to the students in booklet form. In the case of Year 6, this covered the period 1892 to 1924 when all entries for the period were made by the headteacher, Mr Adolphus Herbert Rousham. The retired farmer, Eric Searle, had been taught by Mr Rousham. The students chose particular entries as starting points for exploration. Figure 10.8 shows one from 30 August 1910.

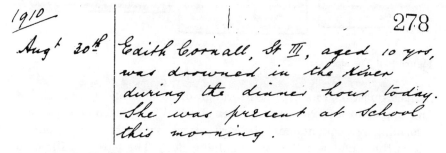

1910   278

Augᵗ 30ᵗʰ Edith Cornall, St III, aged 10 yrs, was drowned in the River during the dinner hour today. She was present at school this morning.

Figure 10.8 An Exwick log-book entry

An enlarged copy was glued to the centre of a large piece of card. The students then identified key questions raised by the entry. We hoped that speculation about the answers would provide convincing detail. The drowning entry prompted such questions as:

> Who was Edith?
> Where did she live and in what sort of family?
> What was she doing down by the river?
> What time of day did she drown?
> Who was with her?
> How did the teachers find out about the incident?
> Who told the family?
> What was said to the other pupils following Edith's death?
> Were new rules established by the headteacher?
> Who found Edith's body?

Individual questions were written above the boxes surrounding the log-book entry (Figure 10.9).

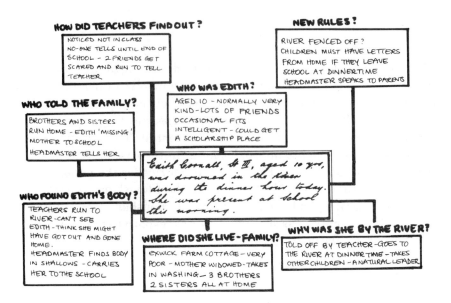

HOW DID TEACHERS FIND OUT?

NOTICED NOT IN CLASS
NO-ONE TELLS UNTIL END OF
SCHOOL - 2 FRIENDS GET
SCARED AND RUN TO TELL
TEACHER

NEW RULES?

RIVER FENCED OFF?
CHILDREN MUST HAVE LETTERS
FROM HOME IF THEY LEAVE
SCHOOL AT DINNERTIME
HEADMASTER SPEAKS TO PARENTS

WHO TOLD THE FAMILY?

BROTHERS AND SISTERS
RUN HOME - EDITH 'MISSING'
MOTHER TO SCHOOL
HEADMASTER TELLS HER

WHO WAS EDITH?

AGED 10 - NORMALLY VERY
KIND - LOTS OF FRIENDS
OCCASIONAL FITS
INTELLIGENT - COULD GET
A SCHOLARSHIP PLACE

*Edith Cornall, St II, aged 10 yrs,
was drowned in the river
during the dinner hour today.
She was present at school
this morning.*

WHO FOUND EDITH'S BODY?

TEACHERS RUN TO
RIVER - CAN'T SEE
EDITH - THINK SHE MIGHT
HAVE GOT OUT AND GONE
HOME.
HEADMASTER FINDS BODY
IN SHALLOWS - CARRIES
HER TO THE SCHOOL

WHERE DID SHE LIVE - FAMILY?

EXWICK FARM COTTAGE - VERY
POOR - MOTHER WIDOWED - TAKES
IN WASHING - 3 BROTHERS
2 SISTERS ALL AT HOME

WHY WAS SHE BY THE RIVER?

TOLD OFF BY TEACHER - GOES TO
THE RIVER AT DINNER TIME - TAKES
OTHER CHILDREN - A NATURAL LEADER

Figure 10.9 The ideas sheet

Each question was explored through discussion and improvisation and as the work progressed, the web of detail grew, each new decision informing subsequent ones. The card served as a working document on which the students jotted down salient ideas. The boxes on the card gradually filled with detail about Edith.

From the work done on the extract, the group decided that Edith was the youngest of five children. Her mother was a widow who took in washing to earn just enough money to keep the family together. On the morning of her death Edith had been told off by the headteacher for not paying attention to her lessons. Rebelling against this, she persuaded a group of her classmates to leave the school yard and, against school rules, accompany her to the nearby river. There, on the bank of the swollen river, they played a game of piggy-in-the-middle with a shoe. When the shoe accidentally ended up in the river, Edith, the strongest swimmer, was persuaded to retrieve it, and in attempts to do so, she was swept away and drowned. At the start of afternoon school, her friends were too frightened to tell their teacher what had happened. When two of them eventually pluck up the courage to report the incident, the teachers run to the riverbank where the headmaster carries Edith's body from the swirling shallows.

These events had power even from the first exploratory improvisations, and the scene which resulted found its way into the play, the children performing it with great skill and sensitivity.

Figure 10.10 Edith's teacher demands to know where she is

Reconstructing lives and events from the past is a matter of considered conjecture based on a careful examination of available evidence. We could only make an educated guess about the background to the drowning. The release of additional information was triggered by the performance. An old lady who came to the play remembered Edith's death. According to this woman, Edith had not waded into the river to retrieve a shoe but to recover her hat, which had been thrown into the water. She would not say who had thrown it in: the perpetrator and our informant will carry that secret to the grave. The children

167

showed great interest in this revelation and were intrigued that their reconstruction had come so close to the reality.

There was a special moment when the children realized the significance of the log-book records to the old school which was to be our performance space. While we stood in the largely unchanged main schoolroom, I read selected extracts from the log-books that described physical features which could still be identified. I read for instance: 'A new curtain rail was fitted to divide the school-room into two'. The children were asked to look for evidence to support this entry: they discovered the original brackets that had held the rail. This process was repeated with entries such as:

> New cast-iron grilles were fitted to the ventilators today.
> Flood water reached to the window sills in the school-room today.
> The cloakrooms near the girls' entrance are to be out of bounds to the boys at all times in future.
> Gas burners were removed from the walls today as our new electric lighting was switched on.

The authenticity of the material we were dealing with was an important aspect of the work. Evaluation was an integral part of the project and Richard Fox, a colleague who looked at language use, comments:

> The school logbook, in itself no doubt prosaic in tone and giving little away, nevertheless was a talisman, which conferred historical authenticity on the events which were shaped into drama. For 9–12-year-olds, authenticity is important, and it is one of the things which makes ordinary objects exciting. Being able to perform in the old school room and to visit the river, the site of the old mill, the war memorial, the graveyard, all these experiences added to the authenticity and to the children's growing realization that they could identify closely with the children they were portraying because they were, in a sense, playing children who had led parallel lives to their own. (Fox, 1990, p.4)

Each of the other groups worked on an extract which had story-making and dramatic potential. In addition to the extract on Edith Cornall's drowning, the others used are shown in Figure 10.11.

Each extract was treated in the way described for the drowning incident. The performance was achieved by joining the resultant scenes together to form a continuous drama. We needed a linking device to give continuity and fit the individual incidents into a coherent storyline, and decided to use a device based on the students' own data collection. We supposed that a group of children who were

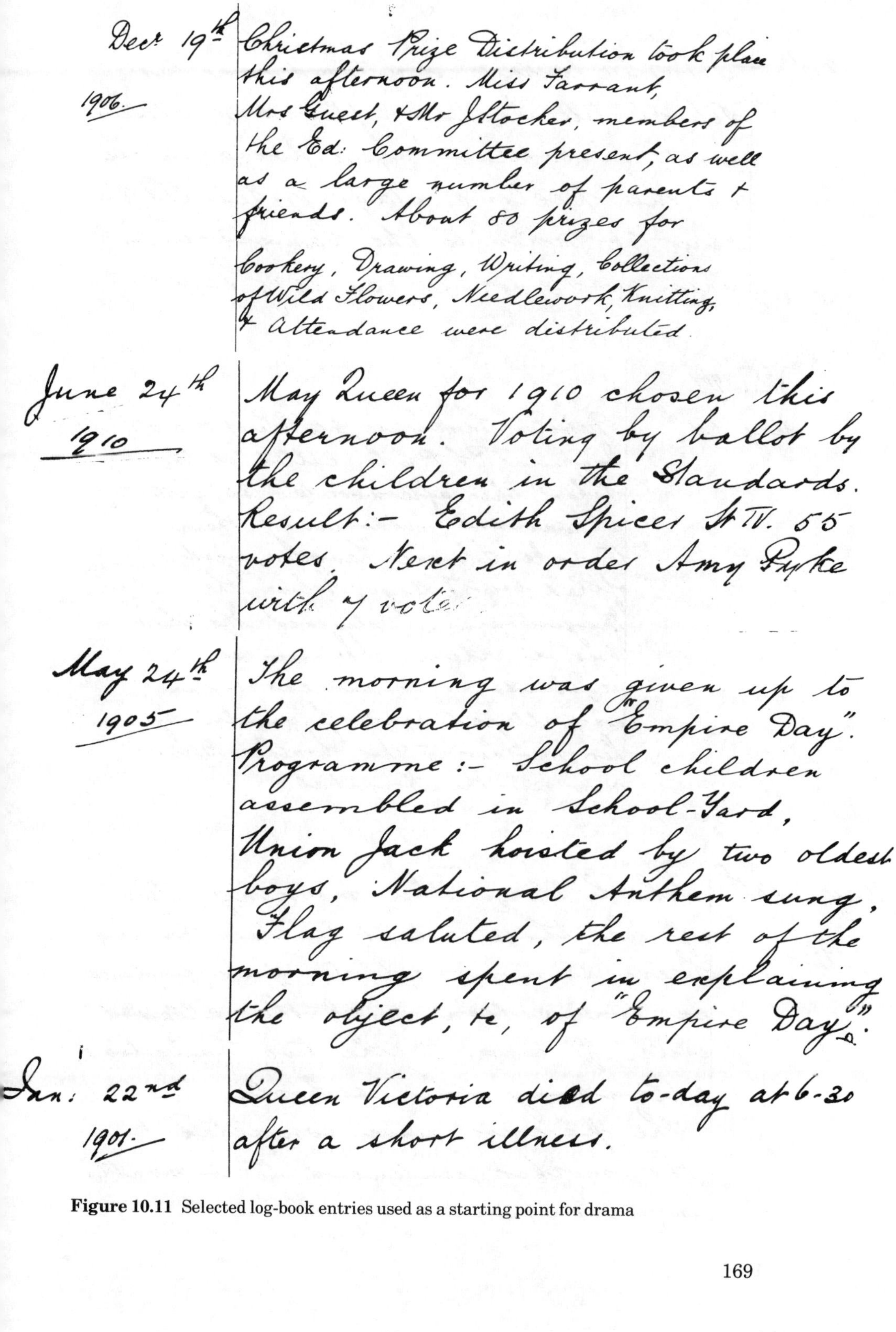

Dec 19th
1906.

Christmas Prize Distribution took place this afternoon. Miss Farrant, Mrs Guest, & Mr J Stocker, members of the Ed: Committee present, as well as a large number of parents + friends. About 80 prizes for Cookery, Drawing, Writing, Collections of Wild Flowers, Needlework, Knitting, & Attendance were distributed.

June 24th
1910

May Queen for 1910 chosen this afternoon. Voting by ballot by the children in the Standards. Result:— Edith Spicer St IV. 55 votes, Next in order Amy Pyke with 7 votes.

May 24th
1905

The morning was given up to the celebration of "Empire Day". Programme:— School children assembled in School-Yard, Union Jack hoisted by two oldest boys, National Anthem sung, Flag saluted, the rest of the morning spent in explaining the object, &c, of "Empire Day".

Jan: 22nd
1901.

Queen Victoria died to-day at 6.30 after a short illness.

Figure 10.11 Selected log-book entries used as a starting point for drama

29th 1916

Dorothy Berry in attendance at School till Friday afternoon inclus:, was discovered by a doctor to be in the peeling stage of Scarlet Fever, & taken to the Sanatorium. This makes two cases of Fever.

127 1901,

May 7th

Detective Parkhouse (City Police) & an Inspector R.S.P.C.C. called at the School this afternoon @ 2.30, with a warrant authorising them to take Florence Langdon, aged 9, of Red Cow Village, before the Magistrates. Delivered the child over to them. She is required as a witness, &c, in an alleged case of cruelty by her mother to her brother Bertie, now in the Hospital.

May 13th 1901.

School closed this morning, two of the three adult teachers having been summoned to give evidence in connection with the alleged cruelty to the two Langdons attending this school. The parents were convicted & the mother sentenced to 4 months imprisonment.

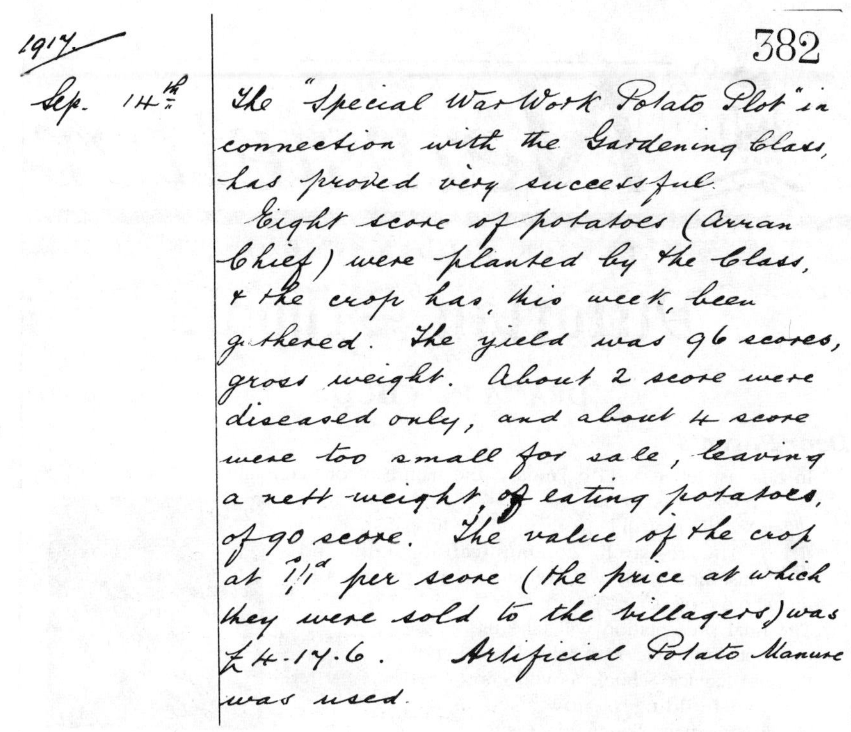

1917.

Sep. 14th.

382

The "Special War Work Potato Plot" in connection with the Gardening Class, has proved very successful.

Eight score of potatoes (Arran Chief) were planted by the class, & the crop has, this week, been gathered. The yield was 96 scores, gross weight. About 2 score were diseased only, and about 4 score were too small for sale, leaving a nett weight, of eating potatoes, of 90 score. The value of the crop at 7/1ˢᵗ per score (the price at which they were sold to the villagers) was £4.14.6. Artificial Potato Manure was used.

Figure 10.11 – *continued*

doing research on local history were going to interview Fred Hanna-ford, an elderly ex-pupil of the school, about memories of his childhood. Fred was played by Gary Read, the only adult actor, who was one of the class teachers involved in the project. The play opened with the children's arrival at Fred's house. After a brief explanation of why they have come they are invited into Fred's home, represented centrally on the set. Their questions set Fred reminiscing on his childhood. As he begins to talk animatedly about particular incidents, the scene cross-fades from his living-room discussion with the children to an enact-ment of what he is remembering – a flashback. Using this device, we were able to build the apparently disparate incidents into a coherent drama. Projected slides, some of them related to album photographs Fred was showing the children, were projected on to screens. Live music, live and taped sound effects, lighting, simple staging, costume and props were used to support the drama. Parents were involved as much as possible in all phases of the production. Regular newsletters were sent home giving progress reports, rehearsal information and asking for assistance. These were produced in the style of the play, with appropriate typography and graphics (Figure 10.12).

Newsletter

EXWICK MIDDLE SCHOOL

𝕭ictorian 𝕾chools

DRAMA IN SCHOOL

2nd February 1990

Dear Parents,

In our last letter of 11th January, the nature of our commitment to the term's project was set out.

We are now able to give you the timetable.

The research, communication skills and historical study will continue as integral parts of the whole project.

The final presentation will take us back to our roots in the Victorian School building of the Old Exwick School. As you know, this building is now used as the Exwick Community Centre.

It is important we rehearse in the building and the Warden has made the following times available to us:

WEDNESDAY - 7TH MARCH - AFTERNOON
THURSDAY - 8TH MARCH - MORNING
FRIDAY - 9TH MARCH - AFTERNOON
SATURDAY - 10TH MARCH - DRESS REHEARSAL
MONDAY - 12TH MARCH - EVENING PERFORMANCE
TUESDAY - 13TH MARCH - EVENING PERFORMANCE

Are **YOU** in this?

Yours sincerely

K. J. Turner
Headteacher

John Somers
Project Leader

Figure 10.12 One of the newsletters

Tickets for the performances – all sold out – took the form of a 16-page programme which contained additional information useful to the audience as context for the drama. Our audience was encouraged to

172

Rule Britannia!

Fred tells the children about one special occasion when Exwick School was visited by Lady Penelope and Sir Dennis - Empire Day! Speeches are made reminding us of the greatness of our country and monarchy, and patriotic songs are sung as the Union Jack is raised. Best of all it means no lessons that day! However, two boys decide they'd still rather be elsewhere.

British, French and German Empires - 1914

British Empire
French Empire
German Empire
German colonies named!

Britain ruled many colonies around the world and during Queen Victoria's reign her Empire flourished. Canada, India, Australia, New Zealand and South Africa were just some of the overseas territories that comprised the British Empire in 1886. This Empire was to expand still further during the next ten years.

The British people were fiercely proud of the Empire that Queen Victoria had built for them.

This patriotic fervour reached the schools each year, on May 24, Empire Day was celebrated. The children would gather, dressed as smartly as they could, and participate in a ceremony to mark the occasion.

Victoria died in 1901.

The Victorian Era had ended.

The Queen had reigned for 64 years and in that time Britain had seen some incredible changes, from electricity to the introduction of the motor-car and the aeroplane. As Queen she had restored the popularity of the monarchy and took her role very seriously. No other monarch had reigned for so long or made a greater impact.

Figure 10.13 A page from the programme

read this before coming to the performance. In this programme (Figure 10.13) we described the factual background to the reconstructed drama.

On performance nights we mounted an exhibition of artefacts, photographs, posters and children's work in rooms surrounding the old schoolroom. Live and taped music and effects were played as people looked at this exhibition, and children in character enacted incidents around the old school and in the playground as the audience arrived. The exhibition was the focus for considerable reminiscing by audience members. As far as was possible, these memories were collected and added to the school's archive. In addition to the public performances, the play was performed to the rest of the school.

The Year 7 radio project – 'I Wish We Were There'

The radio play was to be the culmination of intensive cross-curricular work on the period of the Second World War. The teachers, Carolyn Ballard and Elaine Hennessy, scoured all available sources for relevant materials and extensive use was made of thematic book collections (from the School Library Service), photographic displays, exhibitions of objects (from the School Museum Service and residents), television programmes ('How We Used to Live' and Landmark broadcasts), slides (Exeter before and after the blitz) and recordings (Churchill's speeches and Chamberlain's war announcement). Advertisements and articles were placed in the local newspapers and parish magazine to trace the class of 1938, and valuable leads were established. The vicar was invited in and the students briefed him about the project. He knew a number of residents who had been at the school during the war, and some were still living in the same houses. The admission register for the period was studied to see if ex-pupils could be traced. For a term, the two open-plan classrooms were alive with interesting material, aspects of which constantly changed as fresh research results, new objects and children's work were displayed. Ration books, gas masks, models of Anderson shelters, model aircraft, parachutes and uniforms transformed the areas. The students also contacted their local commercial TV station, which broadcast an item asking members of the class of 1938 to get in touch.

The school wished to compile a permanent archive including photocopies of loaned documents, a collection of photographs, recordings and transcripts of interviews, information gained from questionnaires and a tape/slide sequence comprising key photographs and the reminiscences of residents.

Students used the admission registers to identify and list the evacuees so that authentic names could be used in the improvised drama. They often referred to the log-book entries to cross-reference the material and there was always considerable excitement when oral accounts of events could be verified from written record, and vice versa. Some particularly pertinent finds in the books for years 1925 to 1960 are shown in Figure 10.14.

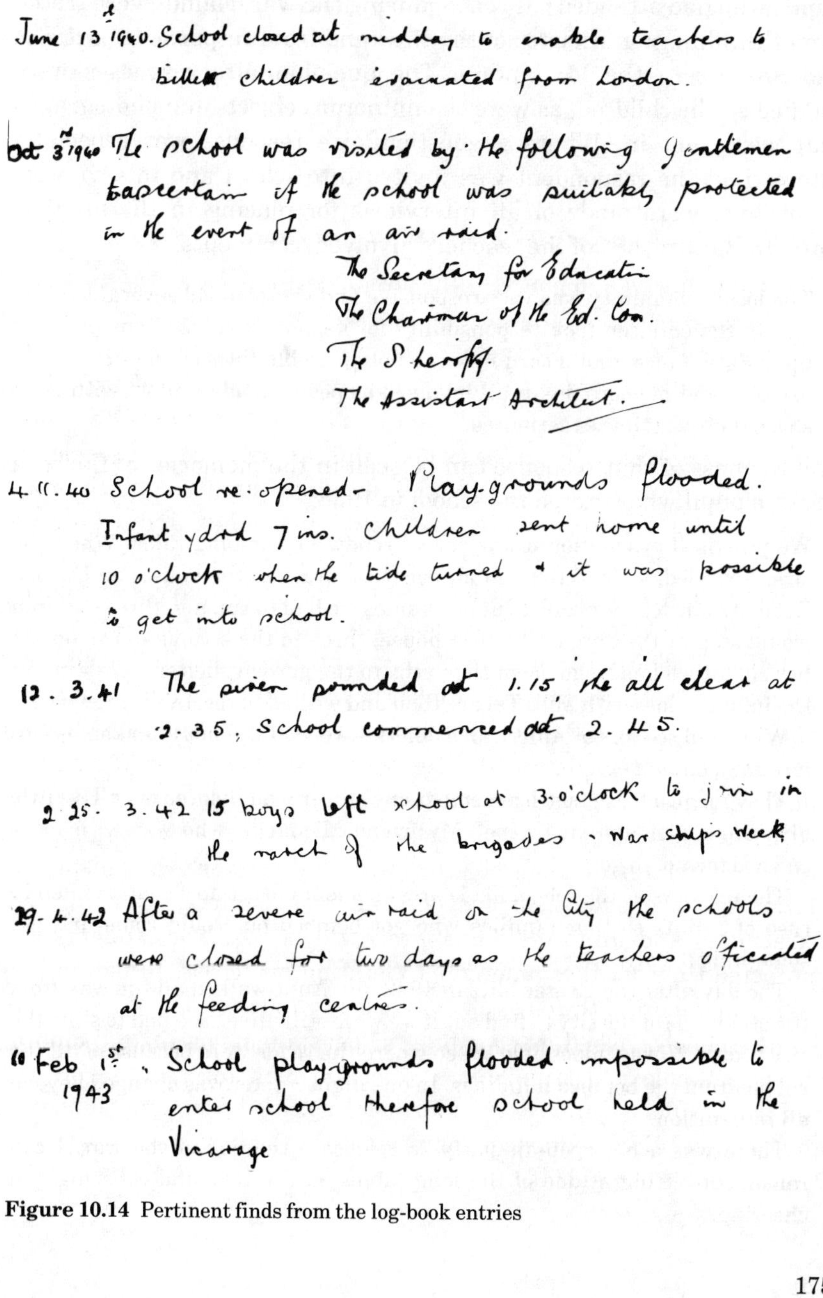

June 13th 1940. School closed at midday to enable teachers to billett children evacuated from London.

Oct 3rd 1940 The school was visited by the following gentlemen to ascertain if the school was suitably protected in the event of an air raid.
The Secretary for Education
The Chairman of the Ed. Com.
The Sheriff
The Assistant Architect.

4.11.40 School re-opened – Playgrounds flooded. Infant yard 7 ins. Children sent home until 10 o'clock when the tide turned & it was possible to get into school.

12.3.41 The siren sounded at 1.15 the all clear at 2.35, school commenced at 2.45.

25.3.42 15 boys left school at 3 o'clock to join in the march of the brigades – War ships week

29.4.42 After a severe air raid on the City the schools were closed for two days as the teachers officiated at the feeding centres.

10 Feb 1st 1943 School playgrounds flooded impossible to enter school therefore school held in the Vicarage

Figure 10.14 Pertinent finds from the log-book entries

Some entries to do with matters such as child abuse and children being sent home for being 'filthy and verminous' could not be followed up because relatives of the children involved still lived in the community. Teachers using log-books in class need to be sensitive to such issues if they are to avoid justifiable complaint.

Year 7 students devised a questionnaire which was targeted at ex-pupils who had attended the school during the war. Names were traced from the admission register of the time and from responses to articles and appeals in the local press. The questionnaire responses were collated by the children, as were the numerous objects and photographs that were sent in. Where a questionnaire response was especially interesting, the respondent was invited into school and interviewed. Recordings were made of all interviews for placing in the archive. Carolyn Ballard, one of the teachers involved, comments:

> The local community was very responsive and we soon had several leads to follow; the children took responsibility for keeping records of our progress up to date. I also kept a card index to note possible lines of enquiry. It was exciting and memorable for all involved as people made contact with us to share their wartime experiences.

The richness of that response can be seen in the memories of Barbara Cross, a pupil who entered the school in 1938:

> We practised evacuation of the school ready for bombing raids. When the siren sounded, we had to go in alphabetical order to the houses on Exwick Road. As our teacher called out our names we had to run and three children would stop at the gate of the first house, three to the second and so on. At her signal we had to go down the paths to the garden shelters. We were in the infants' class with Miss Tucker then and we had to rest every afternoon.
>
> We would see lots of American soldiers – we would shout after them, 'Got any gum, chum?'
>
> They made a fuss of us. I remember one officer who shouted over 'Hi, little girl, come over and sit by me'. My friend Michael – who was with me – warned me not to go.
>
> The teachers at the school made arrangements to set up a soup kitchen in case of a blitz so that families who got bombed out could come and get something to eat.
>
> The day after the Exeter blitz in 1942, my Aunt walked all the way from the other side of the city to find out if we were still alive. She had to skirt the city centre. It was impossible to see where the roads were because of all the rubble from the bombed buildings. In one night Exeter was changed beyond all recognition.
>
> There was a big open-air party to celebrate the end of the war. I can remember sitting at one of the long tables on the Rec. and cheering and cheering.

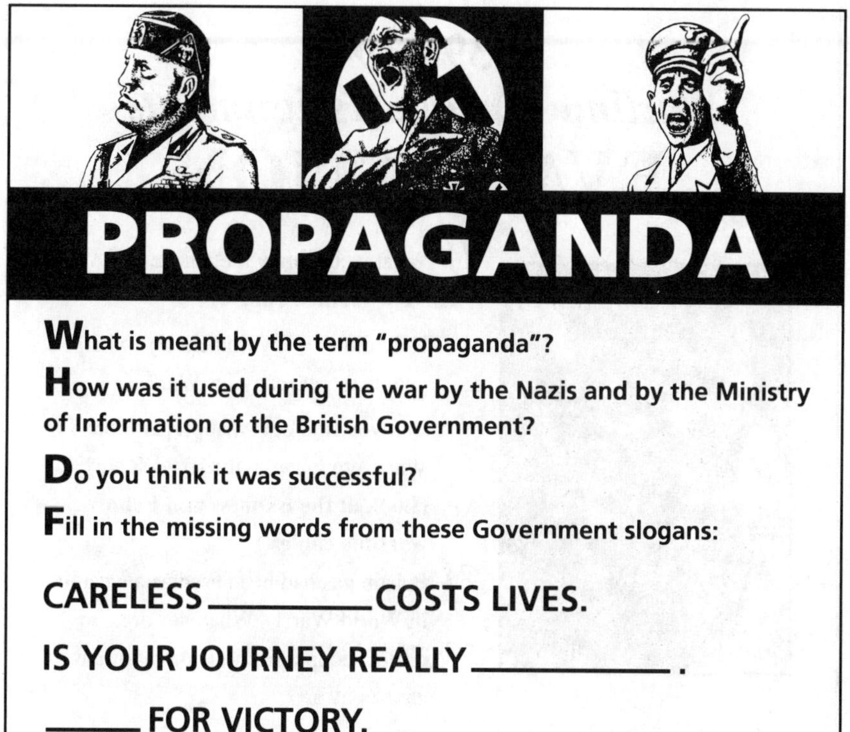
PROPAGANDA

What is meant by the term "propaganda"?

How was it used during the war by the Nazis and by the Ministry of Information of the British Government?

Do you think it was successful?

Fill in the missing words from these Government slogans:

CARELESS ________ COSTS LIVES.

IS YOUR JOURNEY REALLY ________ .

_____ FOR VICTORY.

ALWAYS CARRY YOUR ____ ________ .

COUGHS AND SNEEZES SPREAD ________ .

MAKE ______ AND MEND.

MOTHERS SEND YOUR ______ OUT OF LONDON.

______ HAVE EARS.

Choose a modern issue which you feel strongly about and design a slogan to get your message across.

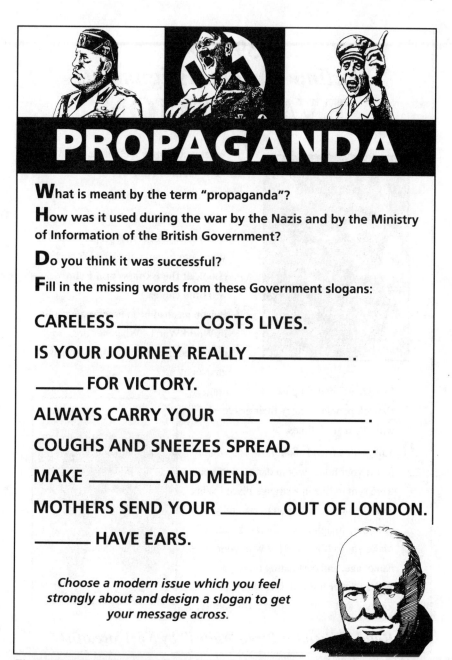

Figure 10.15 Sample assignment sheet

Barbara was shown the log-book and registers and these jogged her memory, which led to the tracing of some of her contemporaries. The students developed a strong sense of being historical detectives and few days passed without them announcing fresh leads. They made good

1939 - 1945
Wartime Britain Assignments
<u>EVACUATION</u>

1) What is meant by the phrase **"The Home Front"?**

How did the Government try to help people to get ready for War?

Can you find out what preparations for War were made in the Exwick are? **(Look at the Express and Echo wartime copies.)**

2) Poison gas had been used as a weapon in World War 1. What was done to protect people from the threat of gas attacks by air?

Design and make a poster to encourage Exwick people to carry their gas masks with them at all times.

3) Talk with a friend about how you would feel if your home was in danger and you were sent to live in a strange place. What would you take with you to remind you of home? Imagine you are an "Evacuee". Make yourself a name tag with your name, age, and destination on it. Write a letter home describing your journey and your new home and family.

Read "When the Siren Wailed" by Noel Streatfield

Figure 10.16 Sample assignment sheet

use of local detail when completing 'Wartime Britain' assignments on evacuation, the blitz, the war effort, further investigations into wartime Britain, women at war, and propaganda. Sample assignment sheets are shown in Figures 10.15 and 10.16.

Students wrote poetry using the incidents described to them by wartime pupils, researched and made wartime recipes and took part in 'make do and mend' sessions which ended in a fashion show for the school. Computers were used to organize, store and eventually present written work.

Developing the drama

Development of the content of the play went hand in hand with learning the skills of radio drama. Early in the process, groups of students attempted a cassette recording of a short scene I had written about the bombing of Exeter. They were aware that the city had been badly damaged in retaliation for the British destruction of Lübeck and the scene posited children watching the bombers swoop in over Exwick as they lined up on the city centre. The script was simple and direct (see Figure 10.17). We decided not to use the standard radio script format at this early stage, preferring to mirror a stage format with which the students would be familiar.

After listening to the results, groups improved the quality of their acting and recording through several more attempts. Their final efforts were shared with the whole group and the teachers drew out the essential teaching points about how to achieve the most effective results. After selecting sections of the log-book, groups improvised scenes suggested through discussion, scripting some of the most successful ones in the style of radio drama. Trial recordings of these were made. Eventually, each group settled on a scene they would like to see in the play. These scenes were based on the log-book entries that follow.

The exploding school boiler

19. 11. 28. At 10.20 a.m. on Thursday Nov: 15th. the front section of the school boiler burst, and the main room has been without heating of any kind until late this afternoon. when the section was. replaced and a fire lit.

The Visitors

Characters: *Florrie, May, Gwen, Billy, Eric, Sid* - all children around 9-12 years old.

The scene takes place in an orchard behind a farm. The orchard overlooks Exwick Village and commands a good view of Exeter. It is late Winter 1942, around six o'clock in the evening. Exeter has suffered a number of recent air raids and lives have been lost and extensive damage done. A group of girls are playing a long-rope skipping game. A group of boys has been bowling hoops down a nearby lane.

(sound of girls playing skipping game in background)

Eric	Bet you can't bowl your hoop under their rope Billy
Billy	Bet I can
Sid	Go on then
Eric	Ready, steady . . . . . .Go! **(the boys rush in after the hoop)**
Billy	Whaaaaaaah . . . . .!
Florrie	You keep off Billy Carter. Go and play somewhere else
Billy	No law is there? We can bowl 'em here if we like
Mary	You're always spoiling our games
Gwen	We'll tell your mum of you **(sound of approaching 'planes)**
Gwen	**(urgent)** Quick, let's get down the shelter
Mary	We haven't got time to run down there, we could get blown up on the way

Figure 10.17 The script used to practise recording skills

Florrie	Under the barn steps, that's where we can go, it's safe there
Gwen	Come on then **(they run to the barn steps)** . . . this is a good place
Eric	Good place! If this lot collapses, us lot'll be strawberry jam
Mary	Oh shut up Eric Davey
Sid	Here they come
Billy	**(jumping up out of hiding)** Ak-Ak-Ak-Ak-Ak . . . **(shouting)** Got you Jerry!
Florrie	Get in Billy Carter, you'll get bombed
Eric	Here . . . . .they're ours!
Sid	No they're not, you can see the swastikas **(sound of planes turning)**
Gwen	They're going for Exeter again
Mary	My dad says it's a sitting target
Billy	Look, Mrs Danby's left a light on - hope they get her
Florrie	The search lights are on **(sound of bomb dropping)**
Eric	Cor, that lit up the Cathedral
Gwen	Blew it up more like **(more bomb sounds)**
Eric	I'm frightened
Sid	Scaredy cat
Mary	I'm going home
Florrie	Let's make a dash for it
Sid	Wait for me!
Gwen	And me!
Billy	**(calling)** Bet you don't make it Florrie Edmunds **(sound of running feet over bombs dropping)**

Severe flooding of the school

12ᵗʰ November. 1950

The Headmistress & the Caretaker entered the School to find all the floors were covered with water & mud, the water having reached a depth of just over one foot as indicated by the water mark on the screen & walls.

The Caretaker, helped by two women cleaners, spent the day washing & cleaning paintwork, bottoms of cupboards, etc. Fires were kept going day & night. No legal documents were damaged. The wireless set & two pianos, although saturated at the bottom, are in working order but require attention & tuning.

Evacuees from Bristol

10.40 During the past week seven evacuees have been admitted to this school, bringing the number to 11. There are seven refugees in the school.

Air raid on Exeter

30.4.42 Normal school. no on roll 120.
During the night of May 3ʳᵈ Exeter received a severe blitz. school was suspended & all teachers officiated at the different feeding centres.

Princess Elizabeth's visit

13.11.46 Medical Inspection — morning.
Children lined streets to see Princess Elizabeth
5 day holiday.

Each scene was finally scripted and bound together. With the agreement of the students, the university students then polished the total offering to enhance its dramatic potential. After much discussion on how these disparate scenes should be pulled together to produce a play, we finally settled on the following structure.

Two pupils have been made to stay in at lunchtime to complete some written work on local history. They are bored, but after the teacher has issued dire warnings about what will happen to them if they don't complete the work while she is at lunch, they reluctantly start to examine some exhibits on the museum table. The first is a piece of the old school boiler which exploded in 1928. They read the log-book entry and begin to imagine what chaos the explosion must have caused. One of them says, 'I wish we were there', and immediately there is a strange warbling sound followed by a scene which builds up to the boiler bursting. We return to the classroom, where the two miscreants think they have had a dream and think no more of it. They move to the second object on the museum table and the use by one of them of the phrase 'I wish we were there' again leads to them witnessing the original event involving that object. This time they cotton on to what is happening and begin to control things, selecting particular objects to trigger their time travel. The teacher returns at the end of the detention period to find two very enthusiastic and knowledgeable youngsters, and she can't figure out why they have changed so radically. The secret remains with the duo, and of course the listeners who are privy to it all.

We held a number of trial recordings in the school, using reel-to-reel tape-recorders, a cassette input for sound effects, a mixer and several microphones. Each recording was evaluated to decide on ways in which the product could be improved. The final script was produced in standard radio drama format, showing the position and duration of music and sound effects. Finally we recorded the play at Devon Air studios in Exeter and it was broadcast in the South-West under the title 'I Wish We Were There' in 1990.

There was a reciprocal relationship between the drama and the curriculum study. The development of the performance fed on material being covered elsewhere, but the drama triggered fresh curriculum study, which in turn fed back into the drama. Classroom work on evacuation led to improvisation of scenes of evacuees arriving in the village, which led to further classroom study of the kinds of language and terminology used at the time – 'That's a fine overcoat you've got there, young shaver'; ration books – gas masks – buzz bombs.

It is likely that this work was taking these 11-year-old students into the realms of Level 5 English. The drama process heightened their

Figure 10.18 Students in the recording studio

understanding of the human consequences of war and because the content of the performance developed from day-to-day curriculum activity, the students had full ownership of the material, a fact which made rehearsal easier, as no explanations of the significance of the content were required.

Reflections

At the end of the project, everyone was left in a state of satisfied exhaustion. The performance and recording requirements had drawn an impressive commitment from each individual and there was a shared sense of having created something significant in terms of both the drama and its effect on the community of Exwick. Gary Read, class teacher to one of the classes involved in the Victorian project, commented after it was all over:

> It was the drama element which enabled us to make the leap from acceptable class teaching to an educational, social and cultural experience the effects of which will remain with those who took part for a very long time.

184

Coverage of specific elements of National Curriculum content had been built in from the outset. Carolyn Ballard conducted a thorough retrospective analysis of the radio project:

> At the outset it is difficult in this kind of project to know exactly all the aspects of the National Curriculum which may be covered. It was exciting to discover on reflection just how many additional attainment targets had been met, confirming a breadth of learning had taken place. The very real context produced high motivation, quality learning experiences and excellent results across the whole curriculum.

The final evaluation showed that, expressed in terms of the versions in force at the time, the research and other curriculum work had covered the following aspects of the National Curriculum:

History

Building up knowledge and understanding of the Second World War; social changes; scientific developments; cultural changes; historical skills.

Programmes of study

KS2 Core Study Unit 4, Britain since 1930, linked to ATs 1, 2, 3 and historical enquiry and communication; local history study.

English

Group discussion; planning and presentation; investigative role play; reading from a variety of sources, fiction and non-fiction, and developing a critical response; information retrieval; enquiry-based reading and analysis; writing for a variety of purposes and audiences; media studies.

Programmes of study

Speaking and listening AT1; reading AT2; writing AT3, also AT4 and AT5.

Mathematics

Investigating problems; measuring ingredients; timing and quantifying in scientific investigation.

Programmes of study

Using and applying mathematics; number; measures; handling data; ATs 1–4, 8, 12.

Science

Planning and carrying out science investigations (plant growth, materials, consumer tests); recognizing the context of scientific development.

Programmes of study

Exploration of science; AT1, also aspects of ATs 2, 5, 6, 9, 10, 17.

Technology

Designing and carrying out technological activities; plan a menu with constraints; producing designs and working with textile and food materials; using graphics for visual messages; present and store information (IT).

Programmes of study

Designing and using artefacts, systems and environments; working with materials; developing and communicating ideas, satisfying needs and addressing opportunities; IT and aspects of ATs 1–5.

Geography

Measuring and recording of weather; mapping bombed areas; change to the landscape caused by human action.

Programmes of study

Geographical skills; places and themes; also aspects of ATs 1–3.

Students would have covered additional National Curriculum areas in the radio side of the work. The Victorian project, in both its development and its performance, covered even more aspects of the National Curriculum. What cannot be wholly evaluated is the value the students derived from experience of recording the play in the radio station's studios and hearing it broadcast to the region, or the pride they derived from the live performance. One pupil commented:

> I felt good when we were doing it for my grandad because he went to my school a long time ago, when it was in the room where we did the play, and he said it was just like that. It's the best thing I've ever done.

It is hoped that the constraints – real or imagined – of the National Curriculum do not impede schools in mounting similar ventures, as they can represent the very best outcomes of imaginative, flexible and professional endeavour.

POSTSCRIPT

Despite my positive attitude to the short-term future of drama in the National Curriculum, I fear for its continued place in a curriculum which appears to have little understanding of and no sympathy for it. Unless teachers fight to retain its culture there is real danger that drama's presence will be diminished as secondary drama specialists are not replaced, its place within English is marginalized and primary teachers are caught up in the 'back to basics' movement.

The New Right orthodoxy would have us believe drama is part of the failed policies of a post-war social-democratic consensus which has contributed to what they perceive as falling standards in education, the family and public life. It may not survive easily in the schools of the next century unless we understand and broadcast its potential to make a unique contribution to the lives of young people. It would take many a ring-binder to balance the scales against projects like the Exwick one.

To strengthen our case, we must ensure that all our drama is of the very best quality, for the key to drama's survival may lie in the enthusiasm of students and the understanding of parents, governors and other teachers.

The only possible resistance to the culture of banality is quality. (Barker, 1986)

FURTHER READING

The following books may be useful if you are looking for ideas. Some are predominantly theoretical in nature (T), others practical (P) and some provide advice on theatre approaches (Th). Those more suitable for secondary work are marked (S), primary (Pr) and for both (G). I have not listed the excellent range of plays which many publishers now offer for use with students of all ages.

Theory (mainly)

Arts Council of Great Britain (1992), *Drama in Schools*. ACGB, London (G,T).

Arts Council of Great Britain (1993), *Dance in Schools*. ACGB, London (G,T).

Bolton, G. (1979), *Towards a Theory of Drama in Education*. Longman, London (G,T).

Bolton, G. (1984), *Drama as Education: An Argument for Placing Drama at the Centre of the Curriculum*. Longman, London (G,T).

Bolton, G. (1992), *New Perspectives on Classroom Drama*. Simon and Schuster Education, Hemel Hempstead (S,P,T).

Day, C. and Norman, J. (eds) (1993), *Issues in Educational Drama*. Falmer Press, London (G,T).

DES (1989), *Drama from 5 to 16*. HMSO, London (G,T).

Hornbrook, D. (1989), *Education and Dramatic Art*. Blackwell, London (G,T).

Hornbrook, D. (1991), *Education in Drama*. Falmer Press, London (G,T).

Jackson, T. (ed.) (1980), *Learning Through Theatre*. Manchester University Press, Manchester (G,Th,T).

Linnell, R. (1982), *Approaching Classroom Drama*. Edward Arnold, London (G,P,T).

McGregor, L., Robinson, K. and Tate, M. (1977), *Learning Through Drama*. Heinemann Educational, London (G,T,P).

Ministerial Drama Working Group (1991), *Proposals for Drama in the Northern Ireland Curriculum*. Northern Ireland Curriculum Council, Belfast (G,T).

Neelands, J. (1984), *Making Sense of Drama*. Heinemann, London (G,T).

Neelands, J. (1990), *Structuring Drama Work*. Cambridge University Press, Cambridge (G,T,P).

Nixon, J. (1987), *Teaching Drama*. Macmillan Education, London (G,T).

Robinson, K. (ed.) (1980), *Exploring Theatre and Education*. Heinemann Educational, London (G,T).

Wootton, M. (ed.) (1982), *New Directions in Drama Teaching*. Heinemann Educational, London (S,T).

Primary

Coulter, B. (1989), *Primary Drama Guidelines, Part 1: What Is Drama in Education?* Somerset County Council, Taunton (Pr,T).

Coulter, B. (1989), *Primary Drama Guidelines, Part 2: Make Believe Play 4–11 Years*. Somerset County Council, Taunton (Pr,T,P).

Coulter, B. (1989), *Primary Drama Guidelines, Part 3: The Structure and Practice of Classroom Drama*. Somerset County Council, Taunton (Pr,T,P).

Davies, G. (1983), *Practical Primary Drama*. Heinemann Educational, London (Pr,P,T).

Stabler, T. (1979), *Drama in Primary Schools*. Macmillan, London (Pr,T).

Whittam, P. (1977), *Teaching Speech and Drama in the Infant School*. Ward Lock Educational, London (Pr,P).

Woolland, B. (1993), *The Teaching of Drama in the Primary School*. Longman, London (Pr,P).

Secondary

Boagey, E. (1992), *Starting Drama*. Collins Educational, London (S,P,Th).

Burgess, R. and Gaudry, P. (1985), *Time for Drama*. Oxford University Press, London (S,T,P).

Burgess, R. and Gaudry, P. (1986), *Time for Drama*. Open University Press, Buckingham (S,P).

Holroyd, R. and Kempe, A. (1993), *Imaging – a Series of Resource Books: Evacuees, The Great Bath Road, A South African Scrapbook, Teacher's Book*. Hodder and Stoughton, Sevenoaks (S,P).

Jones, T. and Palmer, K. (1987), *In Other People's Shoes*. Pergamon Educational, London (S,P).

Lambert, A. and O'Neill, C. (1982), *Drama Structures*. Hutchinson, London (S,P).

Morgan, N. and Saxton, J. (1987), *Teaching Drama*. Hutchinson, London (S,P).

Seely, J. (1977), *Dramakit*. Oxford University Press, Oxford (S,P).

Seely, J. (1980), *Playkits*. Oxford University Press, Oxford (S,P).

Stanley, S. (1980), *Drama Without Script*. Hodder and Stoughton Educational, Sevenoaks (S,P).

Taylor, Ken (ed.) (1991), *Drama Strategies*. Heinemann, Oxford (S,P).

Theodorou, Michael (1989), *Ideas That Work in Drama*. Stanley Thornes, Cheltenham (S,P).

GCSE

Brockbank, K., Marston, P., McGuire, B. and Morton, S. (1990), *Drama 14–16*. Stanley Thornes, Cheltenham (S,P).

Haseman, B. and O'Toole, J. (1988), *Dramawise, an Introduction to GCSE Drama*. Heinemann Educational, Oxford (S,T,P).

Kempe, A. (1992a), *Drama Sampler, Preparations and Presentations for GCSE Drama*. Simon and Schuster, Hemel Hempstead (S,P).

Kempe, A. (1992b), *The GCSE Drama Coursebook*. Simon and Schuster, Hemel Hempstead (S,P).

Shakespeare

Gibson, R. (ed.), *Cambridge School Shakespeare*. A range of plays accompanied by guidance on practical activities. Cambridge University Press, Cambridge (S,P).

Gibson, R. (1990), *Secondary School Shakespeare*. Cambridge Institute of Education, Cambridge (S,P).

Pinder, B. (1990), *Shakespeare – An Active Approach*. Unwin Hyman, London (S,P).

Drama and other subjects

Bird, G. and Norris, J. (1983), *Worlds of English and Drama*. Oxford University Press, Oxford (S,P).

Byron, K. (1986), *Drama in the English Classroom*. Methuen, London (S,T,P).

Fines, J. and Verrier, R. (1974), *The Drama of History*. New University Education, London (G,T,P).

Jordan, C. and Wood, T. (1992), *History Action Packs*. Edward Arnold, London (Pr,P).

Nixon, Jon (ed.) (1982), *Drama and the Whole Curriculum*. Hutchinson, London (G,T).

Wood, T. (1982), *Playback: History Role Plays*. Edward Arnold, London (S,P).

Special needs

Jennings, S. (1973), *Remedial Drama*. Pitman, London (G,T,P).

Jennings, S. (ed.) (1987), *Dramatherapy*. Croom Helm, London (T,P).

McClintock, A. (1984), *Drama for Mentally Handicapped Children*. Souvenir Press, London (G,P,T).

Community theatre

Jellicoe, A. (1987), *Community Plays*. Methuen, London (G,Th,P).

BIBLIOGRAPHY

Arts Council of Great Britain (ACGB) (1990) *Attainment in Drama. Evidence of the Arts Council's informal working group to the NCC.* ACGB, London.

ACGB (1992) *Education – Drama in Schools.* ACGB, London.

Barker, Howard (1986) 'Asides for a tragic theatre'. *Guardian,* 10 February.

Best, David (1990) *Arts in Schools: A Critical Time.* Birmingham Institute for Art and Design, Birmingham.

Black, Paul (ed.) (1992) *Education: Putting the Record Straight.* Network Educational Press, Stafford.

Boal, Augusto (1979) *Theatre of the Oppressed.* Pluto Press, London.

Board of Education (1931) *Report of the Consultative Committee on the Primary School.* (The Hadow Report). HMSO, London.

Byron, Ken (1986) *Drama in the English Classroom.* Methuen, London.

Carpenter, Kenneth (ed.) (1972) *Improving the Lot of Chimney Sweeps.* Arno Press, New York.

Cockcroft, W. *et al.* (1982) *Mathematics Counts.* HMSO, London.

Cox, Brian (1992) 'Curriculum for chaos'. *Education Guardian,* 15 September, p.2.

Croall, Jonathan (1992) *Dig for History.* Southgate Publishers, Crediton, Devon.

Darwell, Elizabeth (1992) *Drama and Curriculum.* Deakin University Press, Victoria, Australia.

Department of Education and Science (DES) (1988) *Education Reform Act.* HMSO, London.

DES (1991) *History in the National Curriculum.* HMSO, London.

DES (1992a) *Education Bill* (71), 30 October. HMSO, London.

DES (1992b) *Choice and Diversity: A New Framework for Schools (Cmd 2021),* 28 July. HMSO, London.

Department of Further Education (DFE) (1992) *Technology for Ages 5–16.* NCC, York.

Devon County Council (1992) *Promoting Quality – Religious Education in the Basic Curriculum.* Devon County Council, Exeter.

Fines, J. and Verrier, R. (1974) *The Drama of History.* New University Education, London.

Fox, Richard (1990) *Evaluation of the Exwick Project.* Unpublished paper available from the author.

Hargreaves, David (1990) 'Planting coherence in secret gardens'. *Times Educational Supplement,* 26 January, p.18.

Her Majesty's Inspectorate (HMI) (1989) *Drama from 5 to 16* (HMI Curriculum Matters, 17). HMSO, London.

HMI (1991) *The Teaching and Learning of Music.* HMSO, London.

Hertfordshire County Council (1983) *Expressive Movement and Dance.* Hertfordshire County Council, Hertford.

Hornbrook, David (1991) *Education in Drama.* Falmer Press, London.

Jellicoe, Ann (1987) *Community Plays.* Methuen, London.

Jones, Nick, Phillips, Martin and Lloyd, Jenny (1993) *KS3. The Shakespeare Play.* Devon County Council, Exeter.

Joyce, Christopher (1990) 'Your genome in their hands'. *New Scientist,* 11 August, pp. 52–5.

Lawton, Denis (1992) *Education and Politics in the 1990s.* Falmer Press, London.

McGregor, L., Robinson, K. and Tate, M. (1977) *Learning Through Drama.* Heinemann, London.

Mayhew, Henry (1950) *London Labour and the London Poor,* ed. Peter Quennell. Spring Books, London.

Ministry of Education (1949) *Story of a School.* HMSO, London.

National Curriculum Council (NCC) (1989a) *English in the National Curriculum.* NCC, York.

NCC (1989b) *Science in the National Curriculum.* NCC, York.

NCC (1989c) *A Framework for the Primary Curriculum.* Curriculum Guidance, NCC, York.

NCC (1990a) *English Non-Statutory Guidance.* NCC, York.

NCC (1990b) *The Whole Curriculum.* Curriculum Guidance 3, NCC, York.

NCC (1991a) *Drama in the National Curriculum.* NCC, York.

NCC (1991b) *Geography in the National Curriculum.* HMSO, London.

NCC (1992a) *Physical Education in the National Curriculum.* NCC, York.

NCC (1992b) *Modern Foreign Languages: Non-Statutory Guidance.* NCC, York.

NCC (1993a) *The National Curriculum and Its Assessment.* NCC, York.

NCC (1993b) *Special Educational Needs and the National Curriculum.* NCC, York.

Nixon, Jon (ed.) (1982) *Drama and the Whole Curriculum.* Hutchinson, London.

Nixon, Jon (1991) 'Reclaiming coherence: cross-curriculum provision and the National Curriculum'. *Journal of Curriculum Studies,* **23** (2), 187–92.

Rattray, K. and Jones, G. (1991) *Drama in the Secondary Curriculum.* Devon County Council, Exeter.

Thomas N. (Chairman) (1985) *Improving Primary Schools.* Report of the Committee on Primary Education. ILEA, London.

Way, Brian (1967) *Development through Drama.* Longman, London.

Willis, Paul (1990) *Common Culture.* Open University Press, Milton Keynes.

Wiltshire County Council (1989) *Topic Planning: A Suggested Approach.* Wiltshire County Council, Trowbridge.

Winston, Joe (1991) 'Planning for drama in the National Curriculum'. *Drama and Dance,* 2D, 11 (Winter), 2–7.

Woodhouse, J. and Wilson, V. (1988) 'Celebrating the solstice'. *Teaching History,* April, 10–14.

INDEX